THE
HALES
BROTHERS
AND THE IRISH REVOLUTION

Dear Dev,

    May we never forget those who sacrificed everything for future generations to have just that, a brighter future.

    Up the Republic,

        Liz

THE
HALES
BROTHERS
AND THE IRISH REVOLUTION

LIZ GILLIS

MERCIER PRESS
IRISH PUBLISHER – IRISH STORY

MERCIER PRESS

Cork

www.mercierpress.ie

© Liz Gillis, 2016

ISBN: 978 1 78117 375 6

10 9 8 7 6 5 4 3 2 1

A CIP record for this title is available from the British Library

Printed and bound in the EU.

DEDICATED TO

THOMAS 'TOMMY' O'REILLY, 1938–2015,

A PROUD CORKONIAN WHO KNEW HIS COUNTY AND

ITS REBEL HISTORY LIKE THE BACK OF HIS HAND.

CONTENTS

ACKNOWLEDGEMENTS

This book has been a long time in the making and over the last twelve years of my research I have been very lucky to have met many wonderful people who were only too willing to share their knowledge with me.

First I would like to thank Mr Seán Hales and his family, Mrs Hales, Anne, Seán and Mrs Eileen Hales McCarthy. You have been so supportive of this book and not only did you give your time generously, you also welcomed me into your home, answered all my queries about Tom and Seán and the whole family, brought me all around West Cork to so many places of interest and were truly amazing. I am indebted to you all for your kindness.

Thanks also to Mary Feehan, who supported the book right from the start, and also to Wendy Logue and all the staff at Mercier Press, and to Jonathan Rossney for his diligent editing and Jennifer Armstrong for proofreading the book.

I would like to thank my college supervisor Dr Bernard O'Connor, Sean Oliver, Mairéad Ní Chíosóig, all the staff and my colleagues at Saor-Ollscoil na hÉireann, and Dr Anne Dolan. To the staff of the Military Archives, I cannot thank you enough: Commandant Padraic Kennedy, Commandant Stephen MacEoin, Private Adrian Short, Corporal Andy Lawlor, Lisa Dolan, Noelle Grothier, Hugh Beckett, Captain Claire Mortimer, Sergeant David Kelly, CQMS Tom Mitchell and Lieutenant Deirdre Carberry. Special thanks to the staff of the Military Archives who have since moved on – Victor, Alan, Chris, Billy and Pat – who were so helpful when I began this project, as well as with all the other projects I have done.

Thanks also to Dan Breen at Cork Public Museum, the staff at Cork City and County Archives, the National Library, the National Archives and Kilmainham Gaol Museum. Special thanks to Councillor John Gallagher, John Brogan, Bernard Warfield, Liz O'Connor and the staff I worked with while in the St Nicholas of Myra Heritage Centre.

Many thanks to Áine Broy, Fergus White, Liam Deasy and family, Con McCarthy, Martin O'Dwyer, Phil Fitzgerald, Seamus Cullen, Brendan Kelly, Dr Mary McAuliffe, James Langton, Henry Fairbrother, Rory O'Dwyer, Diarmuid O'Connor, John Borgonovo, Éamon de Burca (De Burca Rare Books), Meda Ryan, Aengus Ó Snodaigh, Pádraig Óg Ó Ruairc, Ed Penrose, Paul Turnell, Kieran Wise, the National Graves Association and the 1916–21 Club.

To my friends Ruairi O'Donnell, Shane Kenna, Patrick Mannix, Emma-Jane Murphy, Gerry Shannon and Enda Fahy, you have all fully understood my passion with this book and have given me so much encouragement.

Three people that I have to give special mention to are Mícheál Ó Doibhilín, Paul O'Brien and Las Fallon. You are truly fantastic people who have such passion for our history, and I am proud to call you my friends.

To all my family and friends, you have been such a great support to me with this book and I am so lucky that I have you in my life: John, Pat, Mikey, Pheobe, Gerry, Elizabeth, Lydia, Jack, Collette Edwards, and my extended family: Mary, Pat, Brendan, Mary and Rachel Crowe, Catherine Murphy, Derek Horan, Diane O'Reilly, Susan Checkley, Tom Caulfield and Ben Carolan, thank you.

Mimi, you kept me calm and focused many times while writing this book and you are the best big sister in the world. Uncle Pat, you are one in a million.

To my fiancé, James, as always you have encouraged, listened and travelled hundreds of miles with me on my numerous trips to Cork and anywhere else I had to go to write this book; you kept me going and I am truly grateful for your love and support.

Finally to my dad, Mick, who from day one encouraged, supported, searched high and low to get me books, and sat up with up me many, many times into the early hours of the morning listening to me talk about the Hales brothers and anything else I wanted to talk about. You were always there for me and you truly are an amazing dad.

Liz Gillis
2016

ABBREVIATIONS

GAA	Gaelic Athletic Association
GHQ	General Headquarters
GOC	General Officer Commanding
HQ	Headquarters
ICA	Irish Citizen Army
IPP	Irish Parliamentary Party
IRA	Irish Republican Army
IRB	Irish Republican Brotherhood
O/C	Officer in Command
Q/M	Quartermaster
RIC	Royal Irish Constabulary
UVF	Ulster Volunteer Force
Vice-O/C	Vice-Officer Commanding

INTRODUCTION

The first few decades of the twentieth century saw Ireland go through what could be described as a rebirth. At the turn of the century Ireland was a country at the heart of the British Empire, but within twenty-five years she had become a nation in her own right and, although not completely independent of British rule, she had her own government, army, civil administration and police force, amongst other things. This dramatic change from colony to sovereign state was due to the efforts of a generation of Irish men and women who were not willing to settle for the compromise of Home Rule. They were, it can be said, the children of the Gaelic and cultural revival, who wanted complete independence for their country and were determined to achieve that freedom at any cost.

These young men and women, all around the country, joined the various nationalist bodies in their thousands, be they the Gaelic League clubs, Gaelic Athletic Association (GAA) clubs, the Irish Volunteers, the Irish Citizen Army (ICA), Cumann na mBan, Na Fianna Éireann and the Clan na Gael Girl Scouts. The secret oath-bound Irish Republican

Brotherhood (IRB) also experienced a revival of membership, with many young men joining the organisation, the primary aim of which was to gain full independence for Ireland through physical force rather than by democratic means. And in these organisations there was not to be found just one member of a family but, more often than not, many members: brothers, sisters, cousins, fathers, uncles, mothers, aunts, sons and daughters.

The Hales of Ballinadee, Knocknacurra, Bandon, were one such family. Their story in particular epitomises the whole revolutionary period. From the outset, upon the formation of the Irish Volunteers in West Cork, the Hales were involved, and in the years that followed they participated in many pivotal engagements with the crown forces in their home county. They shared not only the successes of battle but also the many hardships that were part of the Irish revolution. By looking at their story in detail, from their earliest years right through to the years of the Irish revolution and its aftermath, I hope to reveal the sacrifices that were made by this generation, and also their families, in their attempts to finally achieve independence from Britain. And by doing so, the question must be asked: was the price of achieving that goal too high?

With regard to the study of the Irish revolution, there are numerous publications on all aspects of the period, be it the Easter Rising, the War of Independence or the Civil War. Equally there are many biographies of the leaders, with Éamon de Valera and Michael Collins being the most popular. In most of these publications, especially when looking at the Civil War period, the reader is sure to find reference to Seán and Tom Hales. But very often their story is told in a few paragraphs. For example, in the three main studies of the Civil War – Michael Hopkinson's *Green Against Green: The Irish Civil War*, Eoin Neeson's *The Civil War in Ireland 1921–1923* and Calton Younger's *Ireland's Civil War* – their story gets only a passing mention.

Even when historians look at Cork's role in the War of Independence and in particular West Cork's role in that war, the Hales brothers are secondary figures. Of course the most famous revolutionary figure from that region, with the exception of Michael Collins, is Tom Barry, commanding officer of the famous Third West Cork Brigade flying column. The Hales brothers are usually mentioned due to their involvement in well-known events, such as Tom's arrest and torture by the Essex Regiment in June 1920, or Seán's role, together with their younger brothers William and Robert, in the Crossbarry ambush in March 1921. Tom Barry, in his autobiography, *Guerrilla Days in Ireland*, and Liam Deasy, in his two autobiographical books, *Towards Ireland Free* and *Brother Against Brother*, do tell their story, but in the wider context of the events that were taking place. However, as Barry and Deasy knew the brothers and fought with them, they are a good starting point from which to look at the Hales family.

The most detailed look at the family as a whole was undertaken by Peter Hart in *The I.R.A. & Its Enemies: Violence and Community in Cork 1916–1923*. As part of the greater narrative, Hart discusses in some detail the family's role in the revolutionary movement in West Cork, dedicating a whole chapter to them. However, with the limited space he had in the book, he gives only an overview of their lives, and because of this the reader does not really see what they sacrificed for the Irish revolution. And that is why I chose to look at their story in detail.

I was always interested in the revolutionary period, but for me the Civil War was what I found most fascinating. Maybe this was due to the fact that when I began to research the period, over twenty years ago, there were not many publications dedicated to that specific subject, certainly not as many as there are today, and while the Hales family was always mentioned, there was no actual book dedicated to them alone. Despite the fact that they were well-known figures within the Volunteer movement and there is a wealth of information detailing their activities, their story, especially in relation to the Civil War, has been somewhat overlooked.

The Hales family, it can be said, symbolises the sacrifices that were made by families who fought in the name of Irish freedom. Of course, the family is not unique in that regard. Many brothers, sisters and cousins fought together in the Easter Rising, War of Independence and the Civil War. One just has to look at the Easter Rising to see many siblings fighting together: the Pearse brothers, the Plunkett family, the Walsh brothers, the O'Hanrahan brothers, the Connolly family, the Cooney sisters, the Quigley sisters and the Henderson brothers, to name a few. But the Hales differ from many of their comrades because as a family they also epitomise the tragedy of the Irish Civil War. Like many families in Ireland, the Hales were divided on the issue of the Anglo-Irish Treaty, but what is unique to them is the fact that two of the brothers, Seán and Tom, were involved in two cataclysmic events that changed the whole course of that conflict: the shooting of Michael Collins in Béal na mBláth in August 1922 and Seán's assassination in Dublin in December 1922, the results of which, even to this day, are still felt in Ireland.

At the time of writing, we are in the midst of the 'Decade of Centenaries'. As the centenaries of the War of Independence and the Civil War approach, it is not enough to know about the events that took place during the years 1913 to 1923. We need to know the people behind those events, those young men and women whose lives could have been very different had they not chosen to fight for the freedom of their country. And it was not just their lives that were affected by the choices they made. They had parents, siblings and, in some cases, children. What did it cost them on a personal level?

It is easy to look back at this time from our perspective in the twenty-first century and say that certain things should not have happened. In recent years it has become common to look at the events that happened in the years 1913 to 1923 and to judge what happened in a way that condemns both the events and, as a result, the people who took part. Unfortunately terrible things did occur, but sadly the harsh reality is that this is the nature of war. To judge these people from our perspective, knowing what we know today, is unfair. These men and women were often ordinary people, living in an extraordinary time. By looking at the Hales family in particular, through their own recollections and that of their friends and comrades, using previously unpublished material and contemporary documents, it is hoped not only to answer the question of what price they, as a family, had to pay for the choices they made, but also to put a human face on their story.

In doing so, the real story, be it one of success, hope, tragedy or all of these elements combined, can be told honestly and without judgement. Most importantly, it should be borne in mind that the men and women of that generation made choices at great personal cost to themselves and their families in the hope of making their country a better place for future generations. That aim, and what these men and women achieved through their willingness to make these sacrifices, should not be forgotten.

1

EARLY YEARS

In the early 1900s no one, either in Ireland or Great Britain, could have imagined that by the 1920s Ireland would have won partial independence from Britain through force of arms. Most Irish people at the time believed that the best they could hope for was Home Rule, a limited form of self-government. This dramatic change was the result of actions by a revolutionary generation who were willing to assert their right to freedom by any means necessary. What made this particular generation different to their predecessors was the central role played by the IRB.[1] Founded in 1858, the IRB, despite many failures in its early years, did not go away or disband. Instead it reorganised and adapted until at last, under the leadership of men like Bulmer Hobson, Denis McCullough, Seán MacDiarmada and, most importantly, Tom Clarke in the early 1900s, it became a cohesive body that brought together many young men who at that moment in time were looking for an opportunity to right the wrongs that had been done to their country by Britain.

The new, invigorated leadership of the IRB realised that if they were to have any chance of achieving the aim of winning independence from Britain, they would need the support of the people – a mass movement. Previous experience had shown that mass movements were capable of achieving goals; for example, Daniel O'Connell and the Catholic Association and their success at winning Catholic Emancipation in 1829, or Charles Stewart Parnell and the Land League and their success at gaining rights for tenant farmers in the late 1870s and 1880s.

The mass movement favoured by the IRB was the Irish Volunteers, an armed militia they were instrumental in setting up in November 1913, ostensibly to safeguard the introduction of Home Rule but in reality to be used by the IRB to win complete independence by force. They were helped by the fact that in the early years of the twentieth century there was a younger generation who were becoming increasingly politicised and questioning the status quo in Ireland. Many of this generation did not believe that Home Rule was the best solution for Ireland and felt that they, the ordinary citizens, would not benefit from its introduction. The most radical young men joined the reorganised IRB, turning it into a more determined and ruthless organisation, and their sense of idealism and belief in a better future for Ireland made a huge difference when compared to the previous failed attempts to win Irish freedom in the years 1798, 1803, 1848 and 1867. In cities, towns and villages all over the country, young men and women sought to play their part in this revolutionary movement by swelling the ranks of the nationalist organisations now available to them.

County Cork, and in particular West Cork, was to play a vital role in the events that took place between 1913 and 1924. The young men and women there had grown up hearing stories of the Famine of the 1840s, which had a devastating effect on that area of the country, most notably in Skibbereen, and of the evictions of tenant farmers in the years that followed, as well as the mass emigrations that took place. These stories helped instil in them a belief that only Irish people, and not a foreign government, should determine Ireland's future, and that future could be achieved only by severing the link with Britain completely. Ironically, it was Bandon, a staunchly loyalist town in West Cork, that found itself at the heart of the revolutionary movement.

Central to this movement was the Hales family of Knocknacurra, Ballinadee, a small townland a few miles outside Bandon. The Hales children grew up hearing stories of England's oppression of Ireland. Their father, Robert, was born in Knocknaun, Cork, in 1849, when the Famine was showing no signs of ending and West Cork was experiencing first-hand the full devastation of this tragedy. The early years of Robert's life no doubt influenced him greatly and helped form his political beliefs. A loyal supporter of William O'Brien, he joined the All for Ireland League and was radically opposed to the landlord system which prevailed in Ireland at the time.[2] It seems he was also, for a time, a member of the IRB.

Robert married in 1867 and with his wife, Margaret, had nine children: Bessie (1874), Anne (1878), Hannah (1879), Seán (1880), Donal (1884), Robert (1886), Madge (1890), William (1891) and Tom (1892). On his farm in Knockna-curra he raised cattle and sheep; he was quite successful at this as his cattle were entered into shows in Bandon and won commendations.[3] Both Robert and Margaret were fluent Irish speakers, a tradition they passed on to their children. Their father's influence would greatly determine the path the Hales children later chose to follow.

On 16 May 1907 Robert Hales' cattle were seized by the sheriff's office because he had failed to pay rent the previous September. Two cows were removed and taken to the Bandon Pound to be sold by the authorities to recoup the money owed. Feeling a sense of injustice at the treatment of their father, Seán and Tom sought to get his cattle back. Together with a number of their friends, they set about planning their operation and were quite prepared to use violence if necessary. Recalling the events of 20 May 1907, Tom Hales wrote:

On one occasion two of my father's cows were in Bandon Pound, behind locked gates and guarded by twenty R.I.C. men. The Sherriff [*sic*] had arrived to proceed with the sale and removal to Cork. About twenty Ballinadee men, armed with ash plants, in a sudden organised attack, scattered the policemen, broke open the gate and rescued the cattle. The police used their batons freely, but the reliable ash plants, weilded [*sic*] by the powerful Ballinadee men, proved better weapons and soon rendered their hands and arms useless. The cattle were, by a pre-arranged plan, driven off to a destination from which the Sherriff never afterwards recovered them. This was an example of combined organisation and physical courage unequalled in those days. The plan was captained by my brother, Seán Hales, in co-operation with the O'Donoghues, Finns, McCarthys, Collins, etc., all of whom were afterwards the leading men in the Ballinadee Company. The above-named were the first in the assault on Bandon Pound; each had a special part allotted to him under the leadership of Seán Hales. Seán and a few others had, of course, a short-term holiday in His Majesty's prison afterwards, and several were on the run for some months.[4]

Because of the raid, Seán and two friends, James O'Donovan of Gallows' Hill, Bandon, and John Deasy of Derrycool, Bandon, were arrested. Seán was detained at around 4 a.m. on the morning of 21 May at his father's home. All three were put on trial at a special sitting of the court in Bandon courthouse on 22 May and charged with 'unlawfully and forcibly breaking into the pound at Bandon and rescuing cattle which were rightfully seized and impounded there by the Sheriff's bailiff'.[5]

The newspapers of the day were full of accounts of the raid. Sergeant McGovern, Royal Irish Constabulary (RIC), who was present at the pound when it occurred, testified in court:

> ... about a quarter to twelve I was standing near the pound gate, which I had under observation. Acting-Sergeant White, Constables Cooper and Kiernan [present also was Sergeant Humphries] were near him [Seán Hales]. The gate was locked. There was a crowd of about a hundred around the gate. I saw John Hailes [sic] in that crowd: he was standing less than a yard outside the pound gate ... The demeanour of the crowd was quiet ... a young fellow who I did not know shoved the gate. There was a rush on the gate then, and it was burst open. About fifty people went into the pound yard and commenced to hunt the cattle. He and the four policemen who were with him got between the cattle and the gate. Acting-Sergeant White and I attempted to close the gate. We were unable to do so owing to the pressure of the crowd. Amongst the people he [Sergeant McGovern] saw James Donovan [sic] and John Hailes. James Donovan was striking at one of the cows with a large stick. He was endeavouring to drive her towards the gate past me. Hailes was pushing the other cow out ... The pound was a scene of tumult. The crowd succeeded in shoving the cows and the police out through the gate. I held one of the cows with Acting

> Sergeant White as long as I could … The crowd successfully
> carried off the cows down the street. They were cheering and
> shouting.[6]

The three men were found guilty and sentenced to two weeks'
imprisonment. This early action was the first indication of
the leadership skills utilised by the Hales during the years of
the Irish revolution.

At this time the cultural and nationalist revival had a firm
foothold throughout the country. Organisations such as the
GAA and the Gaelic League, of which the Hales were members, brought together many young people from all social
classes, and through such bodies they realised they shared
similar political views. Nationalists (Home Rulers), Republicans, trade unionists, socialists and other activists gathered
and talked openly about how a better future for their country
could be achieved. Through these organisations, the first
cohesive steps towards revolution began to appear.

In 1913 and 1914 the establishment of three organisations in particular would help change the course of Irish history: the ICA, the Irish Volunteers and Cumann na mBan
respectively.[7] Of these, it was the Volunteers that would impact on the Hales significantly. William Keyes McDonnell
established the first company of Irish Volunteers in West
Cork on the instructions of the organisation's leader, Eoin

MacNeill.[8] Despite the fact that West Cork had quite a large loyalist population, thus making recruitment for the Volunteers difficult, McDonnell did eventually succeed. The first Volunteer company to be formed was the Kilpatrick Company, and others soon followed.

Tom Hales was the first member of his family to enrol in the Irish Volunteers, in 1913. However, with the outbreak of the First World War in August 1914, his siblings soon followed his lead. 'The family decided they wouldn't join the British Army, so they started up their own company of Volunteers.'[9] Of the nine Hales children, six became involved in the movement: Tom, Seán, Robert and William joined the Irish Volunteers, while their brother Donal, who lived in Italy, later became a Republican Envoy in Genoa during the War of Independence. Their sister Madge, although as Republican as her brothers, did not join Cumann na mBan, as it was safer for her if she was not known to the authorities, who would have been aware of who was a member of Cumann na mBan.[10] This was certainly the case in the War of Independence, when many women were used as intelligence operatives, and in Madge's case, as will later be seen, her role as an arms smuggler between Ireland and Italy meant it was better for her if she had no known connection with Cumann na mBan.

Soon after the outbreak of the First World War the Irish Volunteers, which numbered approximately 180,000 members, split. John Redmond, leader of the Irish Parliamentary Party (IPP), pledged the Volunteers to fight on the side of the Allies during the war, as by doing this he hoped to guarantee the introduction of Home Rule. Many in the Volunteers, especially those like the Hales, who were also members of the IRB, did not agree, believing the freedom of their own country came before the freedom of any other nation.

There were now two groups: the National Volunteers, who followed John Redmond, and the Irish Volunteers, who were still under the leadership of Eoin MacNeill. Although numerically small, many of those now in the Irish Volunteers were seen as radicals and extremists whose only aim was to free Ireland completely from British rule. As a result of the split the IRB had more control over the Irish Volunteers and immediately set about planning the events that would eventually lead to the Easter Rising in 1916.

Early in 1915 the Ballinadee Company of the Irish Volunteers was formed, owing to a request from Seán Hales to Terence MacSwiney, vice-O/C of the Cork Brigade, to come to Ballinadee to organise a company there.[11] Seán had written to MacSwiney, stating:

> They would muster up to 100 men, nearly all over six feet. This sweeping statement caused much amusement but there was something to it, for Ballinadee could rightly boast fine speci-

mens of manhood, with Bob Hales a champion in two counties. The Ballinadee Company was successfully established in 1915.[12]

Soon the Ballinadee Company had earned the reputation of being 'the most prominent ... the best organized, the best equipped and best armed Company of Volunteers in West Cork' and the Hales brothers were at the helm of it.[13] Tom, although twelve years younger than Seán, was O/C of the company and, together with neighbours and friends, built it up from twenty-four men in 1915 to nearly 100 by Easter 1916. The training of the Ballinadee Company began in earnest:

> Parades were held on two evenings a week and a route march on Sundays. These marches were usually to neighbouring towns or villages, and one of their objects was to encourage recruiting for the Volunteers. In this way Sections, some of which afterwards developed into Companies, were organised at Bandon, Kilbrittan [sic], Gaggin, Kilpatrick, Farnevane [sic] and Newecstown [sic], Aiohill and Ballinaspittal [sic]. R.I.C. men usually accompanied these marches.[14]

The Ballinadee Company was not long in building up a cache of arms and ammunition. Each Volunteer was required to pay a subscription of 2d or 3d each week into a company fund for the purchase of weapons and equipment, and throughout

1915 they accumulated arms. In August of that year, seventeen men, fully armed, were chosen to represent the company at Jeremiah O'Donovan Rossa's funeral in Dublin.[15] Tom Hales recalled:

> … P.H. Pearse, who, on his round of inspection came up to us in person that day, and complimented the seventeen riflemen from Ballinadee Company on their symmetrical physique, carriage and discipline. I met him afterwards with others of the I.V. [Irish Volunteer] executive at No. 2 Dawson Street, Dublin. I was told there that Ballinadee was recorded up to then as holding the honour of first place in all Ireland for physique, and second place for discipline, carriage and the marksmanship returns.[16]

On St Patrick's Day 1916 the company took part in the Volunteer parade in Cork city. While returning to Bandon after the day's events, they were attacked by a hostile crowd. Holding their ground, the men fixed bayonets and the mob quickly dispersed. Also in March a parade and exercises were held in Clonakilty and all the local companies attended.[17] The time was approaching for the Volunteers to act and although the majority of the Volunteers were not privy to the actual details of the proposed events, when they did come, the Cork Volunteers, including the Ballinadee Company, would be there to play their part.

2

EASTER RISING

As captain of the Ballinadee Company, Tom Hales was made aware that special operations were planned for Easter Week 1916. On the night of 19 April Tom and his lieutenant, David Collins, were summoned to Brigade Headquarters in Cork city. While there, Brigade Commandant Tómas MacCurtain informed Tom that he was now O/C of the West Cork Battalion and his mission for Easter Sunday was to lead his men to Kilmurray, where they would meet with the Cork City Battalion. Their aim was to procure arms that were due to arrive in Kerry:

> He [MacCurtain] made it plain that this march had a serious purpose. He said we were going to get arms, but did not say at what point. An attempt may be made to prevent our movements, and we may have to fight. But we were to get to the place where we were to meet him at all costs and not to fight unless attacked … I was not to create unnecessary hardship or take out any man who did not know what was before him.

He did not tell me directly that a Rising was fixed for Easter Sunday, but rather left me with the impression that in getting the arms we may become involved in a fight ... MacCurtain told me that our destination on the march was Carriganimma, and that any further instructions would be given by himself or his command at or after leaving Kilmurray if any alteration was necessary. I had no direct information myself and no contact with Dublin at the time, so that I could act only in the light of the instructions given to me by MacCurtain as Brigade O.C.[1]

Also at this meeting the men received a small amount of arms and ammunition. When they returned home to Knocknacurra, Tom disclosed to his brothers what he had been told by MacCurtain. In light of Tom's promotion, Seán was appointed captain of the Ballinadee Company and William was made adjutant. The next day a parade of the company was called, at which Tom informed the men as to what lay ahead:

You have heard from your officers that the muster of the company today is to prepare you for an important route march on next Sunday, Easter Sunday [when] there will be a general mobilisation of the Irish Volunteers ... Ballinadee with the Batt[alion] under my command will march to Macroom, in conjunction with the Batt[alions] from Cork, from there to Carriganime [*sic*], with full equipment to the last cartridge, overcoat and three days rations ... I want no man to march with us on Easter Sunday, or from this day forward, who is not prepared to fight, and risk his life under arms in defence of the cause to which he pledged himself in the Irish Volunteers – the freedom of Ireland.[2]

With this in mind, they began to prepare for the upcoming events. As the week progressed, arms and ammunition were checked and distributed, and unit strength was counted. In the meantime, Cumann na mBan members were busy preparing first aid kits and other necessities for the men.

On Easter Sunday morning, 23 April, the Volunteer companies mobilised at their appointed locations. Ballinadee Company assembled at Brown's Cross at 7 a.m., fully armed. Meeting the various other companies on the way, the battalion reached Kilmurray, where they attended 11 a.m. Mass. Soon after, the Cork City contingent arrived and Seán O'Sullivan took over command of the battalion. As yet no word had been received of Eoin MacNeill's countermanding order.[3] They proceeded to march to Macroom, but before reaching it the battalion was met by MacCurtain and Terence MacSwiney, vice-O/C, who informed them of the countermanding order. A short discussion followed as to what should happen, during which Tom Hales questioned MacNeill's authority to issue such an order. It was decided that the men should proceed to Macroom and then consider their options. Upon reaching Macroom, a 'council of war' was held. The weather had taken a turn for the worse and it was raining heavily. Under such circumstances, it was decided to disband the men. Tom Hales and Chris O'Gorman, captain of 'D' Company, First (Cork City) Battalion, Cork Brigade, were opposed to this and tried to keep the men together and stick to the original plan. A vote was taken and Tom and O'Gorman were overruled. Of the day's events, Tom later stated:

> We came back on the train as far as Crookstown with the Cork Companies and stayed in the village until the early hours of Monday morning. It rained continuously until about 4 or 5 a.m. The Companies then marched back to their own areas. We were very disappointed.[4]

Later on Monday the Ballinadee Company received orders to 'stand to' in their area and immediately the men responded. Under the command of Seán Hales, five houses were taken over by various units, outposts were manned throughout the district, and there the company waited. Orders were sent to all the companies from Brigade headquarters that the men were to 'Stand to arms but don't attempt action against RIC Barracks or military forces until further notice'.[5] This order was hard for all the men of the battalion, not just those of the Ballinadee Company, to understand; they were ready and willing to fight. In response to this, Tom Hales sent a dispatch to HQ in Cork city questioning the delay and the inaction, especially since fighting had begun in Dublin. The reply, however, was the same: 'Under no circumstances to attack Barracks or British military forces without express orders, important definite reasons on part of Brigade O.C. to be made known.'[6]

Seán Hales could not understand this order and proceeded quite angrily to Rathrout, the Ballinadee Company HQ, where 'he gave no guarantee for the further inactivity of his men; when Irishmen were fighting elsewhere, he was prepared to take responsibility for the attack on the two RIC Barracks in the district while there was yet time'.[7] Tom managed to calm his brother down and stopped him from taking any action. On Thursday 27 April Tom sent another dispatch to Brigade HQ:

Taking action on my own responsibility; awaiting [Michael] McCarthy of Dunmanway. If you are in danger of being cut off, send to us a section of your best men, and 40–50 spare Lee Enfield's [*sic*] with ammunition. In face of military cordon I will send transport to get rifles through by secret means. I await your decision, and agreement to this last part.[8]

Although MacCurtain did not support this action, he did not countermand the proposed attack. He made it clear that he would not, however, be responsible for those Volunteers from his command in the city who wished to take part.

It was then decided to make contact with the other companies in West Cork who were willing to fight and join with the Kerry Volunteers in an attack against the British military. In the meantime, the attack on the RIC barracks proposed by Seán was cancelled, as it was deemed to be too dangerous. Any proposed action now rested on word coming from Kerry, but the Volunteers there failed to come out in force. Then, on Friday 28 April Tom Hales received news that there was to be no action from the Cork Volunteers: 'Things had gone too far and we would have no chance.'[9]

In a last-ditch attempt for the company to assert itself in arms, Tom sent yet another dispatch to Brigade HQ urging that at least arms, if not men, could be sent to Ballinadee before it was too late. Nothing came, except for the news from Brigade HQ that the men were to surrender their arms to avoid arrest; the rebellion in Cork was over.[10]

Although Brigade HQ had agreed to the surrender, Tom Hales refused to comply with the order. On 30 April the Ballinadee Company mobilised at Rathrout for their usual training, where they received word that Dublin had surrendered. Both Tom and Seán were there and the parade was watched by two RIC men, Sergeant Crean and a constable, who took note of those present. Tom ordered Volunteers John Corkery, Jack Collins and Denis O'Donoghue to arrest the policemen and take their notebooks, batons and belts. They were released soon after. The incident was not forgotten by Crean, who over the next eight months 'used every effort to harass the men of the Ballinadee Co[mpan]y. And particularly those whom he recognised as being present when he was searched.'[11]

Having released Sergeant Crean, Tom Hales ordered his men to fall in. Seán addressed them one last time:

Each man has played his part, nobly and well, through the stand-to order of the last trying week. Each has proved his metal [*sic*] by his willingness – even eagerness – to take the offensive, if called on. Whatever tomorrow and after may bring, there will be no official surrender from Ballinadee while I am Captain. You will be tried and tested hard by efforts of the old enemy and his agents to break you. Defy and ignore this proclamation for the surrender of arms. Care and love them, they are the sure symbol of freedom. Don't grow despondent, or give way now, unarmed, to the shock of the enemy's offensive – there will be another day.[12]

The men disbanded, but for most the prospects of returning home was not an option, as the British authorities were engaged in mass arrests of Volunteers after the Rising. The Hales, like so many of their comrades, were forced to go on the run.

The month of May began with a series of raids by the RIC in the Bandon area. Seán Hales was identified in Bandon on 2 May but was able to escape. Tom wrote of the incident:

My brother, Sean Hales, was at a pig fair in Bandon on Tuesday, 2nd May, and had scouts on the watch for any movements of R.I.C. or military. He noticed the hasty movements of individual R.I.C. officers on seeing him. He was then on the alert at the top of the Square in Bandon. Suddenly a squad appeared about 150 yards from him. He knew their mission and made off at once across the fields westward. He sent word to me that we would all be arrested and to take no chances. This was double confirmation of my action and of my anticipation of what we may expect.[13]

That night Tom received word from Terence MacSwiney that the company was to disarm; again he refused to obey the order. The following day MacSwiney, together with Seán Hyde, went to Knocknacurra, but Tom was not there. He refused to meet them, but sent word to them warning of RIC activity in the area:

Early next morning the house was surrounded by about 100 military and a force of police; County Inspector Tweedy was in charge. My brothers, Robert and William Hales, wanted to resist, they had two Mauser rifles and some ammunition, but Terry [MacSwiney] would not permit it, and Terry, Robert, William and Sean Hyde were arrested. The two Mauser rifles were captured … The remainder of the Company arms had been put in places of safety. I escaped arrest and did all I could to keep the organisation together.[14]

After their arrest, William, Robert and their comrades were taken to Cork City Gaol. Daniel Hegarty, who was also arrested in the round-up, stated of their treatment:

> We arrived at the Jail at the same time as Terence MacSwiney and the Hales. We had very little exercise during the time we were in Cork Jail. In the early morning of May 9th we were told to get ready. We were put in fours and handcuffed in pairs … There was a soldier with fixed bayonet for each one of us, about 67 I think. We were marched to Glanmire Railway Station with soldiers on each side of us, where we were put on a special train … We arrived in Dublin about 6.30 p.m. and were marched to Richmond Barracks. The conditions there were terrible. We were crowded into barrack rooms without a bit of furniture. Each man got two army blankets, one to put on the floor to lie on and one to put over him. We used our boots as pillows.[15]

Seán was arrested five weeks later. Returning home one night to check on the family, there was a raid at Knocknacurra and he was captured; like his brothers, he was sent to Richmond Barracks. Tom, however, managed to evade arrest.

Robert and William were removed from Richmond Barracks on 12 May and brought to Wakefield Detention Barracks, England, on 13 May.[16] Seán was transferred to Knutsford Detention Barracks, England, on 16 June.[17] Over the coming weeks, in prisons throughout England, the majority of the Volunteers who had been arrested were served with internment orders under the 'Defence of the Realm Act' and sent to Frongoch Internment Camp in North Wales. Approximately 1,800 Volunteers arrived there from 9 June onwards, the three Hales brothers among them, and it was there that the reorganisation of the Irish Volunteers began.

Frongoch has rightly been identified as a 'University of Revolution'.[18] Those interned there were to form the nucleus of what was to become the Irish Republican Army (IRA) in the following years. Interned in the camp were young men, many of whom had not fought in the Easter Rising, but who realised that it had been, as Tom Clarke had said, 'The first successful blow for freedom'.[19] They also believed that if they were to succeed in any way against the British, they would have to fight on their own unconventional terms. These men quickly began the hard task of reorganising.

Frongoch was split into two camps – north and south. Seán was sent to the north camp, which consisted of a number of wooden huts. The south camp was an old distillery. Both elected military staff: 'control of both camps was effectively in the hands of the Irish Republican Army. When all fatigue duties were discharged, military matters began mid-morning with military lectures and drill'.[20] Seán was appointed leader of Hut 3. Frank Hardiman, who was sent to Hut 3, later recorded:

Seán was one of the finest men physically I ever met. It was a delight to see him in his athletic togs tossing half-hundredweights like rubber balls. Occasionally, the late Wm. [William] Mulryan of Kiltulla, Oranmore, another powerful man, with Mick Collins tried their skill with him in weight-throwing and, although giving some splendid exhibitions of their strength, they were no match for Seán.[21]

One of the most important things to happen in Frongoch was the reorganisation of the IRB:[22]

… many Volunteers felt that the goal of national freedom had little prospect of immediate progress. To overcome this defeatist attitude, the secret organisation was set up to rectify matters and the leaders of the I.R.B. in the camp recruited other militants there. Generally they were people of like mind and background. In effect they formed an elite in Frongoch … Henry Dixon and Michael Collins played key roles in this re-organisation which was to establish complete ascendancy over the national movement in the years to follow. It also established Collins as an outstanding leader in those events … It is indisputable that all those Frongoch prisoners prominent in Government and the security forces of the Free State a few years later were the key I.R.B. men in the camp … Joe Sweeney of Donegal says that in Frongoch, Collins was very close to Gearóid O'Sullivan, Seán Hales and Seán Ó Muirthile, three more countymen of Collins, and of course Collins, Hales, O'Sullivan, Ó Muirthile and Sweeney were I.R.B. men.[23]

During their incarceration the men, whether in Frongoch or the various prisons in England, kept autograph books as a memento of their time in prison. In these books some people just wrote their name and the company they belonged to, but others wrote their thoughts and poems that captured their frame of mind. In one such book, Seán wrote:

> Though all the bright dreamings we cherished
> Went down in disaster and woe,
> The spirit of old is still with us
> The[y] never would bend to a foe,
> And Connaught is ready whenever
> The loud rolling tuck of the drum
> Rings out to awaken the echoes
> And tell us the morning has come.[24]

Meanwhile, both at home in Ireland and in England, pressure was growing on the British government to respond to questions coming from many politicians and public bodies relating to the harsh treatment that had been meted out to the Volunteer leadership, and also the continued incarceration of nearly 2,000 men. Of their treatment in Frongoch, Seán wrote:

> The feeding is not sufficient for the ordinary man, indeed far from it ... No one is allowed in here except by going through a

whole lot of formalities and anyone that have [*sic*] not money here is indeed badly off.[25]

Questions were asked in parliament about the treatment of the prisoners. In response to one such query, made in the House of Commons by an MP named Muldoon, in relation to conditions in Frongoch, Seán, incensed that such a man should claim to talk on their behalf, wrote:

Our names have been mentioned in Parliament by some M.P. by the name of Muldoon. How he came to know of us I do not know, but I for one felt humiliated by his asking a question on our behalf, for I would rot here before I would have anyone interceed [*sic*] for my release, that I want to have clearly understood. The principles I am here for are too sacred to be sullied by any false pretence and will under no circumstances avail of any parliamentary intercession for my release.[26]

Frongoch was not only important in the development of the future of the revolutionary movement, it was also the place where strong friendships were formed. This can be seen in the friendship between Michael Collins and the Hales family. Collins had known the brothers before the Rising through Robert, but in Frongoch the friendship was rekindled and strengthened. This was, unknown to them all, to have far-reaching consequences, not just for them personally, but for the whole country.[27]

3

HOMECOMING AND REORGANISATION

By Christmas 1916 all those interned in Frongoch had been released, although a large number of people who had been tried and sentenced were still being held and would continue to be held for a considerable time in prisons in England. For those who were on the run, including Tom Hales, word was received that they were no longer under threat of arrest; they could now return to their homes safely. The internees returned to Ireland as heroes; and no sooner had they returned than reorganisation of the Republican movement began in earnest throughout the country. Tom Hales recalled of that period:

A Ceilidhe was organised in the City Hall for all the released prisoners, which I attended. It was here that I first met Mick Collins. We discussed the future, and the lines on which the organisation was to move. The IRB was to be the main activity, and was to throw in its weight behind Sinn Fein to ensure that it comprised men of grit and energy, until such time as the Irish Volunteers came into the open again.[1]

In the months following the Rising, because of the mass arrests, what remained of the Volunteer companies was disorganised, and Ballinadee Company was no exception. However, it did not take long for the reorganisation to take place, and according to Tom Hales:

From March 1917, the volunteers paraded as a Cycle Corps, and were drilling away again in secrecy. Lectures were arranged for the different groups. Mick Collins had said that County Cork should, in future, have three brigade areas, instead of one. In June 1917, the volunteers were flourishing again, as were Sinn Fein.[2]

There was still a lot of ill-feeling in Cork because of the inaction of Brigade HQ during Easter Week, specifically in relation to the surrender of arms. An enquiry was held in early 1917 regarding the actions of the brigade staff, at which Tom Hales was very vocal in his disapproval of his superior officers:

My accusation against the Brigade Officers [MacCurtain and MacSwiney] at the time was that we had been left in a fog, that arms had been lost unnecessarily and that the loss of arms all over the South was due to the action of Cork. I felt that the same situation could arise again and that something should be done to ensure that the same confusion would not arise. I was hard on the Brigade Officers and both of them felt very keenly about it.[3]

This ill-feeling did not just apply to the brigade staff, as there was also resentment towards those Volunteers who had surrendered their arms. Could these men be trusted in the future? Such was the feeling of discord in the Ballinadee Company against comrades who had given up their arms that it was reduced to less than a third of its original strength in 1916. Even during the War of Independence, when Cork was at the forefront of military action against the crown forces, many men refused to rejoin the company.[4] Despite, this, however, the reduction in membership did not irreparably damage the movement, as those who were still involved were determined that, when the fight began again, there would be no repeat of the mistakes made in Easter Week.

By May 1917 Count Plunkett, father of Joseph Plunkett, urged that Liberty Clubs be established throughout the country. Count Plunkett felt that the organisations in existence at the time were not dedicated to the idea of complete independence from Britain and so Liberty Clubs were set up to provide a political platform for those who wanted to achieve that goal. The Hales brothers were involved in establishing clubs in their area, with Robert stating to Count

Plunkett, 'the men of Ballinadee are heart and head with the movement, and will form a Liberty Club immediately'.[5]

The brothers were keen to form as many clubs as possible and in a letter to a delegate of Count Plunkett, Seán's eagerness can be seen:

> … the Liberty Club was started here on yesterday and I am proud to say that it was started with an enthusiasm and determination of purpose and ideals that left nothing to be desired.
>
> … I may add that we will leave no stone unturned to bring the rest of the surrounding districts within the movement … Men whom I am sure that will get going as quickly as possible to aid us in the venality of those who want to make Ireland a Crown Colony and with no ambitions but the slavish one of Colonial Home Rule.[6]

The Liberty Clubs served their purpose for a time in keeping the spirit of Republicanism alive. But more was needed. With the release of the final prisoners from England in June 1917, reorganisation truly got under way, not just militarily but also politically.

Prior to the Easter Rising Sinn Féin was a moderate party, set up by Arthur Griffith as an alternative to the IPP in 1905. His aim was to achieve something similar to the dual monarchy system that existed between Austria and Hungary, whereby Ireland would have her own parliament, based in Dublin, with control over her affairs, the most important of these being fiscal autonomy. Ireland would remain within the British Empire, which economically would make sense. The point to note is that Sinn Féin, under Griffith, was a non-violent organisation set up to achieve its aim of independence through peaceful means. However, in 1916 the British authorities and media wrongly termed the Rising a Sinn Féin uprising and labelled those involved as Sinn Féiners. While there is no doubt that many supporters of Sinn Féin were involved, the Rising was not orchestrated by the party.

This mistake was to prove costly to the authorities as it played right into the hands of the Volunteers, who were ready and willing to strike another blow for Irish freedom. They knew that if they were to succeed they would need the support of the people and, thanks to the British authorities, they were handed that opportunity with a ready-made political party. The moderate party that was originally Sinn Féin quickly transformed into a militant one with a single aim: complete independence from Britain. It soon eclipsed the IPP as the most popular party in the country and became the political face of the Volunteers. As the popularity of Sinn Féin rose, the Liberty Clubs were amalgamated into the party.

By the summer of 1917 the Volunteer companies had been restructured on a battalion basis. Tom Hales was O/C of the newly created Bandon Battalion, while Seán continued as O/C of the Ballinadee Company.[7] The Volunteers was not the only organisation to undergo great change. Despite the fact that the Military Council of the IRB had been executed after the Rising, the organisation did not cease to exist. Similar to the Volunteers, with its brigades around the country, the IRB had what it called circles, each of which was controlled by a head centre (leader). A circle was made up of individual cells (smaller groups) controlled by an appointed member. The head centre had overall command of his area and would report to the Supreme Council. The IRB and Volunteers soon, it seemed, became one as many commandants and other high-ranking officers in the Volunteers, and later the IRA, were members of the IRB. By this time the number of men being sworn into the IRB had increased dramatically throughout the country. As head centre of the IRB in Cork, and later South Munster, Tom Hales began to swear in new members to the Brotherhood, men whom he knew would be dedicated to winning independence, no matter what.

Reorganisation continued throughout 1917 and 1918 as raids for arms, drilling, route marches and parades by the Volunteers became commonplace throughout the country. However, with the First World War still raging, Britain needed men to fight and the threat of conscription became a reality with the passing of the Conscription Act by the House of Commons in the spring of 1918. The clergy, politicians and the people united to ensure that conscription would not be enforced in Ireland.[8] Men swelled the ranks of the Volunteers; the differences that existed after 1916 disappeared in the face of this threat.

The government reacted strongly to this opposition. The authorities attempted to arrest anyone connected with Sinn Féin, the Volunteers and other nationalist groups. Upon the discovery of the so-called 'German Plot', an alleged conspiracy between Republicans and Germany to cause another rebellion in Ireland, mass arrests of nationalists and Republicans alike took place.[9] Nearly all of the Sinn Féin leadership was arrested. However, many others escaped the authorities, including Seán Hales.

Early on the morning of 18 May a party of RIC men under the command of Sergeant Brennan came to arrest Seán at the family home in Knocknacurra. Tom and their brother William had learned of the impending raid and were staying in Mick Flynn's house nearby. Seán did not heed the warnings. The family awoke to the sound of rifle butts pounding at the door. Their father, Robert, opened it to find ten RIC men and Sergeant Brennan there. Pushing him aside, they called out for Seán to give himself up; his response was that they wouldn't take him alive. A constable was left outside to keep watch for anyone who might come on the scene to try to help Seán. On entering Seán's bedroom the constables tried to handcuff him but, at sixteen stone, Seán was able to resist their efforts.

The whole household was now awake. Present was Seán's younger sister Madge, their cousin Hannah Fitzgerald and her younger brother Michael, who was only thirteen years old. There was no time to lose and in the confusion Madge told Michael to make his way to Flynn's and alert Tom to what was happening. Michael managed to get out of the house unnoticed and made his way to Flynn's, where he told Tom and the others that Seán needed help. Together the four men, Tom and William Hales and Mick and Cornelius Flynn, made their way back to Knocknacurra.

It had gone unnoticed that Michael was missing and on his return he was able to inform Madge of Tom's plan to save Seán. Soon after, the constable who was keeping watch outside saw figures spread along the hillside and could hear them shouting orders to each other. Two other constables were sent out to guard against attack. With little time to lose, Madge and Hannah Fitzgerald informed the police in the house that a whole party of Volunteers was surrounding them. The girls 'also taunted the R.I.C. men with being renegade Irishmen because they were arresting their own countrymen, and they further reminded them that as there were only ten or twelve of them [RIC] present and that there were probably a hundred Volunteers surrounding them they would surely be shot if they tried to prevent the rescue of Seán'.[10] This made the RIC nervous and 'two of them [Constables Kineally and O'Sullivan] actually laid down their arms and refused to take any further part in the attempted arrest'.[11] According to William Hales, they then left the room where Seán was, and the sergeant followed them to find replacement guards. The girls saw their chance and gained entry into Seán's room. Madge whispered to him to make his escape when he heard her close the door of the middle room, which would cut off the access of the two constables who were there and give Seán the time he needed to get out.

Seizing his chance when he heard the door close, Seán leapt up, startling the two constables still in his room who failed to stop him. He forced his way through two more constables and the sergeant at the bottom of the stairs, but Sergeant Brennan made a final attempt to stop him at the door leading into the kitchen. A struggle ensued between the two men, with Seán managing to grab Brennan's gun and take aim. Seeing this, Robert, Seán's father, grabbed the muzzle of the gun and urged Seán to get away. Realising it was now or never, Seán made a dash through the back door and out into the field at the rear of the dwelling house.[12] He had escaped, but a life on the run lay ahead of him.

This escape showed the leadership ability of Tom, as by

spreading himself, William, Mick and Cornelius over a distance, they fooled the RIC into believing they were far more numerous than they really were. The four men pretended to be section commanders, shouting orders to an invisible army, thus securing the escape of Seán.[13]

For months after this the family home was constantly raided by the authorities. In July Tom, William and another Volunteer, Denis Lordan, had a lucky escape. On this occasion the military encircled the house and came upon the three men, who were hiding material they were going to use to make shotgun bayonets. Realising they were surrounded, they made a break for freedom. Under new orders the military had the right to shoot anyone attempting to escape and as 'the three boys made a dash to get away … the military immediately opened fire on them without even calling on them to halt'.[14] They found cover behind a narrow stone fence and, under heavy fire, got away unharmed.

By the end of the year things were changing dramatically within the nationalist movement. The general election of December 1918 saw Sinn Féin win an overall majority of votes, obliterating the IPP and heralding the new spirit of radicalism in the air, showing that the majority of Irish people would no longer tolerate the compromise of Home Rule. The First World War had ended in November and the threat of conscription was removed, resulting in a reduction of membership in the Volunteers. This did little to affect the movement, however; by now there were thirteen companies in the Bandon Battalion alone, making it the largest battalion in West Cork.[15]

As the Cork Brigade was becoming so vast, it was decided to put Michael Collins' suggestion into practice and divide it into three separate brigades. A meeting was held in December where battalion commandants elected the new brigade staff. This restructuring came into effect in January 1919 and training also intensified. Tom Hales was elected O/C of the Third West Cork Brigade, which had six battalions.[16] As a result of Tom's promotion, Seán Hales was appointed O/C of the Bandon Battalion, a position he held until the Truce in July 1921. His younger brother William replaced him as captain of the Ballinadee Company.

January also saw the formation of a new Irish government. The setting up of Dáil Éireann on 21 January 1919 was hugely significant. For over 100 years there had been no parliament in Ireland, as the Irish parliament had been removed with the 1800 Act of Union. But rather than take their seats in Westminster, like their predecessors in the IPP, Sinn Féin instead chose to establish their own parliament in Dublin, Dáil Éireann, thereby representing the people who had elected them in the best possible way. This was also a very symbolic act, not just for Ireland but for all the other colonies under British rule. By doing this they were showing the world that Britain no longer had the right or authority to rule Ireland, and that Ireland was a nation in her own right.

The British government, however, was unwilling to stand by and allow a separate parliament to be established in Dublin. Ireland was ruled from Westminster and that was the way it was going to stay. They refused to release those arrested under the 'German Plot', sticking to their opinion that the Sinn Féin politicians were nothing more than criminals. This action by the British government played right into the hands of Sinn Féin and the Republican movement, and was a huge propaganda victory for them, as it showed the Irish people that Britain was not going to give them what they desired, what they had demanded through peaceful means. The British government, and *only* the British government, would decide and dictate the future of Ireland. But times were changing rapidly, and with their lack of foresight and understanding, and their unwillingness to listen to the people of Ireland, the British government created an environment which would only increase the tension that already existed. For at that time there were many men and women who were waiting for their chance to strike another blow against Britain, and now the government had given them that opportunity.

As Dáil Éireann was not recognised by the British government, it had to find a way of financing itself. From August

1919 the Volunteers were involved in organising and collecting for the Dáil Loan. Michael Collins, as Minister for Finance, was authorised to raise funds, and a loan was set up whereby people, both in Ireland and abroad, most notably America, could buy bonds which would gain interest once the government was recognised internationally. Their aim was to raise £500,000, both at home and abroad. By September 1920, when the loan ended, the amount raised in Ireland alone was £370,163.

The most significant event in 1919 was the handing over of control of the Volunteers from their own independent Executive to Dáil Éireann. As the legitimate army of the Irish Republic, now embodied in the Dáil, each Volunteer swore an oath of allegiance to defend the Republic and its government, Dáil Éireann. From that time on the Volunteers became known as the Irish Republican Army – the IRA.[17]

4

1919–1920: FIGHTING FOR INDEPENDENCE

The War of Independence began on 21 January 1919, the same day Dáil Éireann was formally established in the Mansion House, Dublin. At first, attacks were centred on the RIC throughout the country by local IRA units, and a policy of boycotting the force was enforced and supported by the population. However, the year was mostly spent preparing for what was to come and, as 1920 approached, the war intensified as the IRA became more organised and efficient as a fighting unit.

As O/C of the Third West Cork Brigade, Tom Hales had the authority to sanction actions against the crown forces and throughout this period he, Seán and Robert Hales were involved in numerous attacks on the authorities.

On the morning of 25 February 1920 a party of Volunteers under Seán's command attacked the RIC barracks in Timoleague. Men from the Ballinadee, Timoleague, Clogagh,

Ballinspittle, Barryroe and Kilbrittain companies took part in the engagement. It was planned to use a mine to breach the building but it failed to detonate. The IRA then opened fire and tried to explode the mine by setting alight a load of hay at the barracks door, but that too failed. The fight raged for some time but was eventually aborted and the men returned home.[1]

Two days later Tom, with about forty men, led an attack on Mount Pleasant RIC Barracks. Again the plan was to use a mine to breach the building, but the attack failed because the RIC heard gunshots before the mine could be laid. This operation was the first to be sanctioned by IRA General Headquarters (GHQ) in Dublin.[2] Initially, engagements against the crown forces, military and police were carried out on the orders of the local command. However, in early 1920, with the increase in attacks against the authorities, GHQ in Dublin felt that control was needed throughout the country and it was decided that all future operations should be submitted to headquarters for approval. Due to the nature of the war it was not always possible to follow this protocol, but in all cases reports of engagements were given to headquarters in the aftermath of such activities.

In May a party of Volunteers under the command of Tom made an attempt to ambush an RIC patrol making its way from Bandon to Mount Pleasant. They were in position all day but the RIC never showed. Also that month Tom led an ambush party that lay in wait for a patrol of British military at Killowen, but again the military did not appear.[3]

On 2 June the Cork County elections were held, in which Seán Hales and a number of Republicans were elected to the Rural District Council. Also in that month Dáil Éireann authorised the setting up of Republican Courts, directly undermining the authority of the established courts throughout the country. They quickly gained the support of the people and proved to be very capable of administering justice. Seán Hales was involved in cases put before the Bandon court and according to one source was 'a natural lawyer and conducted the proceedings with great competence'.[4]

In July Seán was in charge of a company of eighteen men who attempted to ambush a military patrol at Killavarig, near Timoleague. Again the patrol failed to appear.[5]

As 1920 progressed, the war became more brutal, due mainly to the arrival in Ireland of two newly created British forces – the Black and Tans and, later, the Auxiliaries. The Black and Tans, under the command of General Tudor, were sent to reinforce the RIC all over the country, as the constabulary were becoming less and less effective in their operations against the IRA. The Auxiliaries were a completely independent force, under the command of Brigadier General F. P. Crozier, and were a small unit, numbering approximately

1,500 men in all. They were a counter-insurgency force, concentrating on utilising intelligence and very ruthless methods to try to destroy the IRA. These forces were posted throughout Ireland, including Cork. In addition, in West Cork, another unit, the Essex Regiment – to be exact, 'D' Company of the Essex Regiment – under the command of Major A. E. Percival, were merciless in their opposition to the IRA. Over the coming year these units, especially the Auxiliaries and the Essex Regiment, became synonymous with terror, murder and torture throughout the West Cork Brigade area.

It was not long before the Essex Regiment scored a significant victory against the Republicans with the capture of Tom Hales and Pat Harte, quartermaster of the Third West Cork Brigade, on 27 July 1920. At 8 a.m. that day, Detective Sergeant William Mulhearn had been shot and killed by two members of the IRA outside St Patrick's Catholic Church, Bandon, on his way to morning Mass. Originally from Mayo, Mulhearn was the chief intelligence officer of the RIC in West Cork and was very efficient in carrying out his duties. He was responsible for many raids and arrests of IRA men in the area, and therefore became a target of the local IRA. An attempt had already been made to assassinate him in March 1920, but he managed to escape. Despite his taking precautions, the IRA continued to observe him, resulting in his death on 27 July. It is unclear whether or not Tom had anything to do with his actual assassination, but as O/C of the Third West Cork Brigade, it is unlikely that he did not sanction the attack.

Because of the death of Mulhearn, the crown forces carried out a series of raids on known Republicans in the area. Hales and Harte were captured at Hurley's farmhouse at Laragh, near Bandon, where they were due to meet Liam Deasy, brigade adjutant, and Charlie Hurley, vice-commandant of the Bandon Battalion. They were standing outside the house when it was suddenly surrounded by police and military, leaving them no means of escape. An army officer approached and asked who they were, so both gave him false names. Hales and Harte were brought into the farmhouse by the military, where they were stripped and searched. Incriminating documents were found on Tom and, with their hands tied behind their backs, both men were brutally beaten. They were then dressed, placed in a lorry and taken to Bandon Military Barracks. Tom Hales later wrote of their treatment:

> We were taken to Bandon into the Military Barracks yard and were lined up to be shot. The soldiers were howling for our death and were anxious to shoot us. We had our backs to the wall and Harte was on my left hand side.

… We were still tied with our hands behind our backs, and the soldiers hit us with their fists. My sight was getting very dim owing to the blood that I was losing and I felt very weak.

… [Captain] Kelly paced out 12 to 15 paces from us, and then put five or six men with rifles at the end of the 15 paces. Harte was then very weak and could hardly see. He [Kelly] stuck a flag into Harte's hand and made him hold it up. I recognised that the flag that Harte was holding up was the Union Jack, but Harte himself was too far gone to recognise it. A man came with a camera and took a snapshot.[6]

They were then taken to a room and later interrogated separately. Hales continues:

About midnight I was led out by a guard and taken to an upper room. There were, I believe, six officers in this room including: —

Captain Kelly of the Enemy Military Intelligence Department, stationed at Cork City.

Lt. Keogh of the Hants Regt.

Lt. Richardson in charge of Wireless at Bandon.

Lt. Green, believed to be of the Hants Regt.

They were sitting down as though they were going to try me. There were no soldiers only officers in the room.

Kelly opened the proceeding[s] by saying 'We are going to try you'. My hands were still tied behind my back, and the strap was fastened round my neck and face.[7]

Captain Kelly proceeded to question Tom. Upon refusing to swear an oath on the Bible that he would answer their questions in full, his bare legs were whipped with canes. Kelly was aware of Tom's identity, knowing the rank that he held in the Third West Cork Brigade. As the interrogation continued and he refused to give the information the military wanted, Tom was again severely beaten. The interrogation then centred on Tom's brother Seán; again he refused to speak:

> He [Kelly] said, 'What position does your brother John hold and where is he staying?' I said, 'I refuse to give you any information about him'. He then turned to the Officer whom he had sent for the pliers, and he started bending and twisting and pinching my fingers at the back. He gripped them at the back placing one portion of the pinchers against one side of my nail and the other portion of the pincers against the other. He brought the blood to the tops of several of my fingers, and for some time afterwards my fingers were black on the tops owing to the congealed blood there.[8]

More questions followed, as did the torture, but still Tom refused to speak. Eventually the interrogation came to a close. But before he was removed, he again received a terrible beating at the hands of Lieutenant Keogh:

> Keogh hit me several times in various parts of the body, but

especially in the face, and he broke the four front teeth in my upper jaw. He then knocked me down on the ground. I was absolutely exhausted and nearly fainted, and my senses were beginning to go. He hit me on several occasions while I was on the ground. After a few minutes one of the officers said, 'That's enough'. I was then dragged up and lead [*sic*] out of the room.[9]

Harte was then brought into the room for interrogation, where he received the same treatment. The following morning the men were taken to a yard where they were told they were to be shot. At the last moment, the authorities changed their minds and the men were instead brought to the Military Hospital in Cork. Tom recalled that at the hospital they were treated well and their injuries tended to. They were later moved to a ward 'where there were twelve wounded policemen and they were all day and all night long talking at us and crying for our blood. This had a very detrimental effect on Harte who, in consequence, is now in a very weak mental state'.[10]

On 20 August the men were tried by court martial and were sentenced to two years' hard labour. Tom was initially sent to Dartmoor Prison in England and later transferred to Pentonville Prison, where he eventually recovered from his injuries. Because of his treatment during the interrogation, Harte had a mental breakdown. However, the authorities refused to believe that he was in such a state of poor health and also incarcerated him in Pentonville Prison, which no doubt had a further damaging effect on him.

On their removal to prison in England, Michael Collins immediately organised for Art O'Brien, the Dáil's Republican Envoy in London, to arrange for his men to visit Hales and Harte at every opportunity and report on their welfare. It was on one such visit that Tom gave his statement to J. H. MacDonnell (Mac) of their treatment after their arrest. Collins insisted on getting this information as it would prove to be very useful as propaganda. The statement was published and sent to Republican Envoys all over the world. It was published, in its entirety, in the American Commission.[11]

Art O'Brien wrote to Collins about Harte on 6 October 1920:

Since writing you the first memo, a friend from Sagart has come in. He tells me that a Dr Dyer (who is not an independent specialist, but is on the Home Office staff), visited Harte, and after making an examination, it was agreed that Harte should be left as he is for one month, and kept under observation, in order to see how he goes on. Evidently, the Governor at Pentonville has some idea that Harte is shamming … Sagart thinks it possible that Harte may be certified insane, and also thinks that, if representations were made to the Home Office, stating Harte had responsible friends, who were willing to look after him, outside, that he might be handed over to them …[12]

The correspondence between Collins and O'Brien is quite sad in relation to Harte. The letters are now held in the National Archives in Dublin.[13] Over a period of two years, they show that Harte suffered extreme mental distress because of his torture, that there was absolutely no hope of him recovering from his ordeal and that all his comrades could do was to try to get him home. It seems that the prison authorities were reluctant to transfer him, as the letters show by January 1921 he was still being held in Pentonville. Eventually they did agree to have Harte transferred, although the exact date is unknown, and by June he had been removed to Broadmoor Criminal Lunatic Asylum (now Broadmoor Hospital).

An interesting point to note was that according to O'Brien's contact Mac, Captain Kelly, who had been one of the main perpetrators in the interrogation and torture of the men, actually visited Harte while he was a prisoner in Pentonville. O'Brien, in a letter to Collins on 7 September 1920, wrote:

> Hales says that through ill-treatment Harte is a little bit unbalanced. This might account for his attitude to MacDonnell, who saw him yesterday. MacD. could get very little from him indeed. He did not seem to be satisfied with your note of introduction and would not talk. MacD. subsequently found from Hales, that it was not he (Hales), who had been visited by Capt. Kelly, but Harte. Harte had said nothing about this, but

when Mac heard it from Hales, he asked for Harte again, and Harte admitted that it was true, but said that he did not attach very much importance to it. Mac asked him exactly what were the words used by Capt. Kelly and Harte said that the words used were:– 'I am here to specifically charge you with the murder of Sergt. Mulhern' (or Muldoon), he could not remember which.[14]

Pat Harte never did recover from his ordeal. Even after the Treaty was signed and the majority of Republican prisoners were released, his family had to wait nearly two months before he was set free. In early February 1922 Harte was finally brought home to Ireland and was admitted to the Richmond Asylum in Dublin. Despite receiving the best possible treatment, he died in 1924.

With Tom now in prison, Charlie Hurley replaced him as Brigade O/C, and Liam Lynch, O/C of Cork No. 2 Brigade, took over as head centre of the IRB in South Munster. Before Tom's arrest it had been decided that the brigade was to intensify activities against the crown forces. On 29 August 1920 Seán was in charge of a party of Volunteers who were planning to ambush an RIC military patrol at Brinny. Various companies from the Bandon Battalion were involved and the men were in position from 27 August. Unknown to them, their movements were reported to the authorities and the ambush failed as the military, knowing that the

Volunteers were lying in wait, came upon them from the rear and opened fire on them. The main body of Volunteers managed to escape, but Volunteer Tim Fitzgerald of Mount Pleasant Company was killed in the attack.[15]

Before the formation of the Third West Cork Brigade flying column, thirty-seven officers, including Seán Hales, took part in a training camp at Clonbuig at the end of September. Their aim was to become an elite fighting unit that could attack the military quickly and withdraw with as few losses as possible whenever an opportunity arose. The men trained for ten hours a day, drilling, signalling and practising attack and defensive exercises. The column was divided into four sections, with a section commander in charge of each one. The Third West Cork Brigade flying column came into existence at the end of September under the command of Tom Barry. Over the next year it proved itself to be a force to be reckoned with.

On Tuesday 5 October the flying column assembled to attack a party of the military on the Dunmanway to Bal–lineen road. Seán Hales was in charge of the Bandon Bat–talion section. The flying column, sixty men in all, waited all day, but the military did not appear. For another two days the Volunteers waited for the military, but they never showed. On Thursday it was decided to disband the column temporarily. The weapons were needed for another training camp and so Seán was placed in charge of the column and ordered to take the men to Newcestown with the arms, ready for transfer the next day. On Saturday 9 October the column reached Coolenaugh, Newcestown. Seán dismissed the men and the majority of them made their way to billets in the surrounding area, while fifteen men found lodgings in Lordan's and Corcoran's houses in Newcestown. Seán and his vice-O/C, Jim O'Mahony, went into Newcestown village and while they were there two Crossley tenders full of members of the Essex Regiment arrived. The two men managed to escape unnoticed and sent word to the Volunteers billeted in Lordan's farmhouse.[16] John Lordan, captain of the Newcestown Company, quickly regrouped the column and led his men towards the village. But before reaching it they came upon the two tenders, which had just left Newcestown, and opened fire on them. The fight at Newcestown Cross lasted approximately half an hour, during which time Seán and Jim O'Mahony had managed to locate the column. When the fight was over Seán ordered his men to fall back. The column withdrew having suffered no losses. The Essex Regiment's losses were two officers killed and three wounded.[17]

On 24 October the Toureen ambush took place. Toureen was located on the main road between Bandon and Cork, and was a road frequently used by the military, making it an ideal location to mount an attack. Seán was a section commander in this engagement. The attack was over in minutes and the IRA was successful in capturing a number of arms while suffering no losses. The British, however, lost five men, with four wounded.[18]

On 21 November a brigade council meeting was held in Gloun. Many prominent members of the brigade column were present, including Seán Hales. When the meeting ended, each party set about returning home, but on the way three of the groups, which were initially travelling in the same direction, were stopped by a patrol of Auxiliaries at Coppeen. The first two groups, which included amongst others Richard (Dick) Barrett, brigade quartermaster, Charlie Hurley, brigade O/C, and Liam Deasy, brigade adjutant, were searched. Soon after, Seán Hales' party arrived and was also stopped and searched. Con Crowley and John O'Mahony, who were accompanying Seán, had incriminating documents on them and were taken prisoner by the military. In what was fast becoming a tense situation, Seán gave a false name, John McCarthy, and told the officer in charge, Colonel Crake, that he was buying cattle in the area. Surprisingly Crake believed him, even going so far as to say, 'I believe what you tell me. You have an honest face, and if all your countrymen were like you, there would be no need for us here.'[19] Crake was killed one week later in the Kilmichael ambush carried out by the West Cork Brigade flying column under Tom Barry, one of the most successful engagements undertaken by the column in the War of Independence. In the end, everyone except Crowley and O'Mahony was allowed to continue on their way.

In early December Seán ordered the destruction of Timoleague Castle, the RIC post at Timoleague and the house of Colonel Travers. Timoleague Castle was due to be taken over as a military outpost, while Colonel Travers' residence was to be commandeered to house members of the military. The IRA could not allow this to happen as increased numbers of enemy forces in their midst would hamper their activities. Daniel Donovan, a member of the Clogagh Company, Bandon Battalion, who took part in the operation, wrote:

> During the first days of December, 1920, I was sent by the Battalion O/C (Seán Hales) to the Brigade Q/M (Dick Barrett) to collect explosives required for the demolition of Timoleague Castle which, it was rumoured, was about to be occupied by enemy forces. I collected the explosives in Crosspound area and took them by a roundabout route to Clogagh, taking them later in the same week to Timoleague area where preparations for the operation were being made. On the same occasion the evacuated R.I.C. post at Timoleague, and the house of Colonel Travers, which was also due for occupation by the enemy, were due to be destroyed. The combined operation was carried out by representatives from Clogagh, Barryroe, Timoleague

and Kilbrittain Companies. All buildings were completely destroyed.[20]

One of the main problems faced by the IRA was its lack of weapons and, more importantly, ammunition to carry on the war. Arms were regularly smuggled into the country from Britain and other locations, but always in small quantities. Often this work of procuring and smuggling weapons was undertaken by women, including Madge Hales. Madge's involvement was not known to the authorities and she would often pass on secret messages to Michael Collins from her brother Donal in Italy:

> She [Madge] was a key link in the arms importation and carried many of Mick's [Michael Collins] instructions in her head. Often her brother [Donal] would write to her and she would travel to Dublin by train from Cork to convey the message to Mick. She was also in a position to decode some of Donal's ambiguous statements in his letters to Collins. Madge was the link between Collins and Liam Deasy and his Third West Cork Brigade, members of which were involved in preparing dumps for the arms.[21]

Donal Hales had been for many years living in Genoa, where he had gone to teach before the First World War, finding work both in public and private schools. On the outbreak of the war, he publicly aired his views regarding his opposition to Italy taking part. In 1919 Donal was appointed 'as a Consular and Commercial agent in Italy for the Irish Republic' by Ernest Blythe, who at the time was Minister for Trade and Commerce in Dáil Éireann.[22] This came as a result of an article that Donal had written for the Italian press in which he highlighted what was happening in Ireland. Michael Collins had seen the article and was so impressed by what he read that he asked Blythe to contact Donal and offer him the position as trade agent in Italy. Through his contacts in the Italian press, Donal became one of the main Republican propaganda agents in Europe and regularly published articles relating to Ireland in both the national and local papers. Every week he received reports from Collins with news of the week's events in Ireland, which he would then report in the Italian press: 'We showed that England, who was pretending to be a civilised country, was simply assassinating the inhabitants of a civilised and civilising country like Ireland.'[23]

Aware of the chronic shortage of arms, in November 1920 Cathal Brugha, Minister for Defence, sent Seán Ó Séaghdha (John Patrick O'Shea) to Italy to see about arranging a shipment of arms. Ó Séaghdha recalled:

In addition to the instructions, Cathal also gave me a letter of introduction to Donal McHales [*sic*] of Genoa (Agente

Consolare Generale, Irlandese per L'Italia. Piazza S. Bernando 26, Genoa, or Via Montesuello 3-10) …

I recall how eager Donal McHales was to give me all the information as to how I could get in touch with the War Office official in Rome to discuss the purchase, delivery and packing of the military equipment.

… Donal wasted no time in taking me to the War Office official's place of reception … an order for the military equipment was given and instructions as to its packing, such as, a false bottomed ship which was to transport the equipment. Having made arrangements for the purchase of the arms … we probably interviewed shipping firms and purchased quantities of marble and architectural work in Genoa which was to act as camouflage for the arms.[24]

In December Madge went to visit Donal in Genoa in relation to the arms shipment. Months passed, but no arms were sent from Italy. Madge returned to Italy in mid-1921 to see her brother and relayed to him what Collins had told her. Donal recalled:

My sister spoke to Collins then who said the money would present no difficulty at all. He mentioned the sum of £10,000 which she thought would be sent immediately. No money was sent and they [the arms] were never removed.[25]

As 1920 drew to a close, the acts perpetrated by both sides had increased in savagery and it seemed that there was no end in sight to the fighting. Like many conflicts, things would have to get much worse before they got better and over the next six months the Hales family was central to those events.

5

JANUARY–JULY 1921

Although the brigade flying column had been disbanded temporarily for a much-needed break before the end of 1920, this did not mean that the IRA rested on its laurels. Planning was afoot for the first action against the military in 1921. The Bandon Battalion, under the command of Seán Hales, was to attack the RIC barracks in Kilbrittain, but as the barracks was a heavily fortified structure a mine was needed if there was to be any chance of success. On the night of 2 January the attack took place but, as in previous engagements, the mine failed to explode. Rifle fire soon erupted, and, realising that the barracks was not going to be captured, the men withdrew.[1]

By 16 January the brigade flying column had been re-formed, and members of the Bandon Battalion, again under the command of Seán, were making their way to join it in Rossmore. On the way they came upon a party of the Essex Regiment in Quarry's Cross. Fighting ensued but the company was led away successfully, having suffered no losses.[2]

Keeping up the momentum, plans were put in place to attack Bandon RIC and military barracks. Under the leadership of the column commander, Tom Barry, it was proposed to launch a three-pronged attack to draw the military out from the protection of the barracks and engage them in open combat. The attack took place on 24 January and members of the Ballinadee Company, including its captain, William Hales, were present. The column encircled the town and shortly after midnight the fight began. It lasted two hours, during which the military never left their stronghold. On the orders of Tom Barry, the various sections of the column were told to withdraw. Later, as the day wore on and the column regrouped, it was discovered that they had suffered one loss – Volunteer Daniel O'Reilly from Kilbrittain had been killed in the attack.[3]

January had been a very busy month for the West Cork Brigade and the brigade flying column. They took the offensive and attempted to ambush the military at every opportunity. In February the brigade suffered heavy losses, as some Volunteers were arrested and others were killed in action. As a result, morale was low amongst the men. Despite these blows, however, they remained determined in their efforts to keep the pressure on the enemy forces. What was needed was a large-scale engagement, and both Tom Barry and Liam Deasy were putting into action their plans for the next phase – an ambush on the Essex Regiment. By this time it had been observed that the military no longer ventured out in small groups but rather travelled in large convoys. To have any chance of mounting a successful assault, the brigade flying column would have to be brought up to full strength.

On receiving intelligence on 16 March that a considerable number of military personnel were to be sent to Bandon from Kinsale as reinforcements, it was decided to ambush them midway at Shippool. The column was in position from the early hours of 17 March but, as the day progressed, it became clear that the military were not going to arrive. To ensure their safety, the column withdrew to nearby Skeough and remained in billets until the following evening. The next night it was decided to move the column to the main Cork to Bandon road, near Crossbarry, where it was almost certain they would engage the military. The column was divided into seven sections. Seán Hales was in charge of Section 'A' and with him were his brothers Robert and William. Each section went to their respective billets nearby, ready to assemble at any moment.

In the early hours of 19 March word came through of an extensive encircling action by the military. The column quickly mobilised and paraded before Tom Barry, who told them what was afoot. Although they were expecting to come across a large number of military, they had no idea as to the actual numbers they were about to face. Troops from the Essex Regiment, the Hampshire Regiment and the Auxiliaries were in the raiding party. In all, the column, which numbered 104 men, was set against a force of approximately 1,200. Each section commander led his men to their allotted positions:

> All sections were allocated to positions north of the Cork–Bandon road where the road ran east to west for a distance of approximately seven hundred yards. The sections under Seán Hales, John Lordan, Pete Kearney, Mick Crowley took up positions behind the roadside fence and in the farmyards of the Harold and Beasley families … The strength of each section was about a dozen. All were armed with rifles.[4]

With each section in position, the column waited. Between 7.30 and 8 a.m. lorry loads of military came into view. Soon the sound of rifle fire from John Lordan's Section 'B' reverberated throughout the area; they were the first shots of the 'Battle of Crossbarry', a fight comparable to that between David and Goliath. Section after section opened fire and 'within ten minutes of the opening of our attack we had smashed the British encircling lines wide open'.[5] Eventually the firing ceased. Three lorries had been caught in the initial gunfire and many troops were killed and wounded. The Volunteers were successful in capturing a Lewis gun, rifles and ammunition, and were ordered to destroy the lorries.

Flor Begley, assistant brigade adjutant, was instrumental in raising the morale of the men at Crossbarry, as Liam Deasy recalled:

> He [Flor Begley] had followed my suggestion made a few nights previously that he should bring along his war pipes in honour of St Patrick's Day. He had the pipes with him now, and as soon as the shooting started he began to play rousing war tunes which could be clearly heard during pauses in the rifle fire. The stirring marching airs brought life and encouragement to the Volunteers in their grim struggle. This was Begley's finest hour and one on account of which he will be ever remembered as 'The Piper of Crossbarry'.[6]

The fight soon resumed as the military continued with their encircling movement. However, each section of the column continued to attack them successfully.

Eventually the order was given to withdraw. Each section commander knew the route to take, and Seán Hales led his column away while one section was left to cover the rear. After a long route march, the column made its way safely to Gurranereagh, twenty miles west of Crossbarry, on Sunday morning. The 'Battle of Crossbarry' was over.

In all, 104 Volunteers had fought their way out of an encircling movement containing approximately 1,200 fully trained soldiers. The column did not escape unscathed, as

IRA losses were three killed and two wounded.[7] According to the IRA, British casualties were 'thirty-nine soldiers killed, including five officers, and forty-seven wounded'.[8]

One reason why Crossbarry was such a successful engagement was due to the leadership displayed, not only by Tom Barry but also by the section commanders, including Seán Hales. They had led their men, some of whom had never before been under fire, to victory against overwhelming forces, proving to the British authorities that the IRA was indeed a force to be reckoned with.[9]

The column did not have any time to enjoy their success as a follow-up engagement had been planned. The RIC barracks in Rosscarbery was a thorn in the side of the IRA in West Cork. The authorities believed it was impenetrable as it was heavily fortified with a machine-gun post. The attack took place on the night of 30 March, and Robert Hales was a member of the attacking party. A mine was placed at the barracks door and it exploded, breaching the barracks. It also caused a lot of damage to nearby houses. A fierce battle ensued. Although it was impossible for the column to make any advance into the barracks itself, under heavy fire they proceeded to douse the building with paraffin and set it alight. The fight lasted nearly five hours, after which time the RIC was forced to abandon the barracks:

To do this they were obliged to jump from the top window to the ground. A few escaped to Clonakilty about 9 a.m. and reinforcements arrived to find the attackers gone and most of the small garrison dead or wounded. The killed were Sergeant Shea and Constable Bowles; seriously wounded: Constables Doyle, Kinsella and Harken; wounded: Head Constable Neary, Constables Bradley, Woodford, Sullivan, O'Keefe and Roberts. The remainder were unhurt. No arms or guns were lost.[10]

The column, having achieved their objective, moved off having suffered no losses. They made their way to Newcestown, after which the column was again demobilised.[11]

At the end of April Seán's section of the brigade column was stationed near Clogagh. He received word that a transport of military was to arrive by train between Courtmacsherry and Ballinascarthy. Plans were put in place to ambush the transport:

Positions were taken up on the railway embankment a short distance from Timoleague Railway Station by the men of the column reinforced by men from Ballinadee, Timoleague, and Clogagh Companies ... When the train arrived at the ambush position there were no military on board, so the men from the column withdrew to billets and the men from the local units returned to their home areas.[12]

By May 1921 the Cork Brigade, overall, had suffered heavy losses due to the execution policy adopted by the British. As a result of martial law having been declared, the authorities had the power to execute people for several different offences, including being in possession of arms.[13] In early 1921 a number of IRA men from all over the country had already been executed. On 14 March alone, six IRA men – Patrick Moran, Frank Flood, Patrick Doyle, Thomas Whelan, Bernard Ryan and Thomas Bryan – were executed in Mountjoy Gaol. In response to this the IRA ordered a general 'shoot-up' against the military, which was set to take place on 14 May. Warnings had been sent to General Strickland, GOC of the martial law area, Cork, that if the executions of IRA men did not stop, reprisals would be taken against his forces. Strickland ignored the warnings.

At 3 p.m. on 14 May all ten garrisons of enemy forces in West Cork were to be attacked. Of the engagement at Innishannon, Con Flynn wrote:

> … arrangements were made for a party consisting of Jack Corkery, Bill Hales and Tim McCarthy – all from Ballinadee Company – in co-operation with some men from Innishannon unit to ambush a patrol of RIC at Innishannon on May 14th 1921. The Battalion Adjutant (Jim O'Mahony) was in charge of this operation, in which one member of the enemy patrol was killed. The IRA had no casualties.[14]

On 28 May it was planned to ambush the Auxiliaries at Gloundaw, between Drimoleague and Dunmanway. The brigade column was mobilised and similar to the tactics used at Crossbarry, the column was divided into sections, one of which again was under the command of Seán Hales. However, the column's movements were seen and betrayed to the Auxiliaries, who proceeded to plan an encircling movement, with reinforcements coming from Bantry and Skibbereen. The column withdrew successfully, eventually reaching Caheragh, where it was disbanded.[15]

In June it had come to the attention of the brigade staff that hundreds of British reinforcements were to be deployed to their area and billeted in both Bandon and Skibbereen workhouses. Plans were quickly made to destroy the workhouses. Seventy members of the brigade column were mobilised and split into two – one party under the command of Tom Barry would go to Bandon, the other group under the command of Liam Deasy would go to Skibbereen.

In both instances arrangements were made to safely house the occupants of the workhouses before the IRA set about the task of destroying the premises. Seán Hales was one of the officers involved in the destruction of Skibbereen workhouse and it was in flames in less than an hour. With the objective achieved, the column withdrew to safety.[16]

For some time the crown forces, backed by the government, had been enforcing an 'official' policy of reprisals, destroying local businesses, and in many cases houses, of either known IRA men or their sympathisers. There were of course many 'unofficial' reprisals carried out by the crown forces and to counter this Brigade HQ proposed that the IRA would do the same to the property of pro-British supporters. In response to the policy of arrests and court martials of IRA men being carried out by the crown authorities, it was also decided that prominent pro-British supporters should be taken hostage. Previously this policy had not really been adopted because it was not ideal for the IRA to remain in one location for any length of time guarding a prisoner. Doing so would have meant that they ran the risk of being discovered by the authorities, so it was not seen as a feasible option. The reality now was that those in IRA custody would have to be executed. However, with the escalation of arrests and executions of IRA men, they were left with little choice. Time was of the essence and, determined to show the authorities that this was not an empty gesture on their part, the West Cork Brigade set their sights on a very high-profile target.

Seán Hales was ordered to destroy Castle Bernard, the residence of the Earl of Bandon. It was a formidable residence situated just outside Bandon town and had been in the Bernard family since the mid-1630s, during the Munster plantation. Over the centuries the family became very wealthy and powerful landlords, and in 1800 Francis Bernard was awarded the title of Earl of Bandon.

The Earl of Bandon at this point, and the fourth holder of the title, was James Bernard, who had inherited the title upon the death of his father, Francis Bernard, in 1877. He had been married the previous year to Georgina Evans Freke, daughter of Lord Carbery. His time as earl was not as successful as his father's. It was the time of the Land War, when the rights of tenant farmers were being fought for by Charles Stewart Parnell, Michael Davitt and the Land League. Farmers on the Bernard estate either could not or would not pay their rents and so the estate fell into financial difficulty. Lord Bandon, determined not to be defeated by the Land League, set up the Irish Defence Union to protect the interests of the landlords. He was elected to the House of Lords and was chairman of the Bandon Town Commission. The Bernards were known for throwing lavish parties, but they were living beyond their means. To keep up their lifestyle the earl was regularly forced to sell off valuable family items to cover his costs. Eventually it became too expensive to run the house and by the time it was attacked, it had fallen into a state of decay.

The earl was also lord lieutenant of Cork, but it seems he was not highly regarded as such. During the War of Independence he was publicly criticised in the press by Bishop of Cork

Daniel Cohalan for not speaking out against the behaviour of the crown forces. According to *The Cork Examiner*, the bishop stated: 'Lord Bandon is Lord Lieutenant of County Cork but he may as well be Lord Lieutenant of Timbuctoo for all the good he does for his people.'[17]

In the early hours of the morning of 21 June, Seán Hales led a party of nine Volunteers into the grounds of Castle Bernard. This was a very dangerous operation as it was known that there was a party of military posted in the grounds of the castle each night: 'Commandant Hales decided that the party would proceed to the Castle and endeavour to take the Earl of Bandon as a hostage even if it was necessary to fight our way in and out.'[18] They reached the house and knocked on the door but there was no response. Attempts were made to enter the house forcibly but that failed. In the meantime, Volunteer Denis Lordan, who was posted at the rear of the house, gained entry through the conservatory and let the attacking party in. Upon initially searching the property no one was found. According to Denis Lordan:

Commandant Hales then decided (to use his own words) 'as the bird has flown we will destroy the nest'. No preparations had been made to burn Castlebernard [*sic*] and we simply piled up some furniture in a few of the rooms and put the curtains from the windows over it and set fire to the curtains.[19]

The Volunteers continued to search the premises and soon enough the earl and his household were discovered. Lady Bernard, wife of Lord Bandon, later wrote of the events that night:

> The way they treated us was like the French Revolution … The head man [Seán Hales] was so insulting to me, saying there is no Lord Bandon and that the likes of us had ruined the country. Thank God I kept my head and prevented them being rough to B. (Lord Bandon) when he tried to struggle with them.[20]

The attacking party took Lord Bandon as a hostage, then quickly withdrew and took their prisoner to a secret location. At about 8 a.m. an armoured car arrived on the scene but it was too late, as the house was ablaze and the earl was nowhere to be found. The fire brigade arrived soon after and despite their efforts, they could not save the building. As one witness noted, 'The ruin is absolute and all one can do is to wander across the masses of debris in those precious rooms.'[21]

Over the next few days there were many similar attacks by the IRA on such houses in the Bandon and Innishannon districts.

The destruction of Castle Bernard was for Seán, understandably, too good an opportunity to miss, considering that his family home and all their belongings and farming equipment were deliberately destroyed by the crown forces in early March 1921. Nothing but the four walls of the house was left standing.

Soon after the attack, General Strickland received word that the IRA was holding prominent pro-British supporters hostage. With it came the warning that unless the executions of IRA prisoners stopped, these hostages too would be executed. Having been kidnapped, Lord Bandon was held in numerous safe houses in Barryroe. The military searched day and night but could not locate him. He was, it seems, treated well by his captors. Donal Hales later wrote:

> When my brother, Seán, burned Lord Bandon's Castle as a reprisal for the burning down of our house, Lord Bandon made him a present of a fine stick, as a mark of his gratitude and esteem, for Seán's conduct towards him and for saving his life.[22]

The kidnapping of Lord Bandon had the desired effect. As a result, pressure was put on the British government to end the conflict. The Earl of Midleton, who was a cousin of Lord Bandon, was most vocal in this. No more executions took place and a little over two weeks later, on 11 July 1921, a truce came into effect at 12 p.m. The next day, 12 July, Lord Bandon was returned safely to his estate, which now lay in ruins. Hostilities between the Irish and British forces ceased – the War of Independence was over.

However, what lay ahead of the Volunteers was more dangerous than anything they had faced before. It turned brother against brother and tore the country apart. No one could escape, least of all the Hales family, what was about to unfold – the Irish Civil War.

6

TRUCE AND TREATY

When news of the Truce was announced there was, under-standably, great joy and relief amongst the ordinary civilians all over the country. For over two years they had watched as their cities and towns were destroyed and they had, as in all conflicts, suffered greatly during that period. Éamon de Valera and General Macready, General Officer Commanding-in-Chief of the British forces in Ireland, had held talks in the Mansion House in Dublin on 8 July 1921, at which it was decided that hostilities would cease on 11 July at 12 o'clock. As a result of the Truce coming into effect, curfews were to be lifted and, although attacks by both sides were to end, both armies could continue to train and drill.

For those who had been fighting the campaign, the Truce was received with mixed emotion, on both sides. The British forces felt betrayed by their government. By parlaying with the IRA the British government, although not declaring it publicly, recognised the IRA as a legitimate army and the Dáil as the legitimate representative body of the Irish people. With regard to the untried Volunteers being held in prisons and internment camps all over the country and in Britain, they were to be granted prisoner-of-war status. For those who had been fighting what they referred to as 'murder gangs' only months before, this was too much.

Seán Kavanagh, who was in Mountjoy Gaol at the time, recalled:

> I was in Mountjoy with a few hundred other chaps when I heard about the truce. That was really the victory of the whole thing. [Richard] Mulcahy always maintained that … the truce was the most significant thing in the war against the British at that time because it was they that asked for it, not us. They had called us murder gangs, and now they wanted to treat with us as a legitimate army and government. I don't think we could have carried on much longer without it. It gave us a kind of breathing space to train more Volunteers and purchase more arms for a resumption of hostilities, if necessary.[1]

This was, it seems, the opinion of most Volunteers. The Truce was *not* the end of the fight; hostilities, they assumed, would resume at some point and when that time came they would be ready to renew the campaign. They would use the Truce for their benefit, or so they believed. As future events proved though, this was not to be the case.

Tom Barry had been appointed chief liaison officer for the martial law area which included Cork. In this role he was to liaise with British officers to ensure that both sides were adhering to the terms of the Truce. He was aware of the attitude of the British forces towards him and his colleagues, and felt that they had to be vigilant. He believed that the men had to remain alert and, above all, they *must* remain a disciplined fighting unit. But, as he later stated:

> The truce went on for six long months, and I feel it was deliberately calculated by the British to drag it out as long as they could. They were used to dealing with subject races, and they knew very well that a long truce is always bad for the weaker force. They knew that our morale and effectiveness were bound to deteriorate over a long period. All the British forces in Ireland … they were all housed in barracks, they were paid, dressed and fed. But what was our guerrilla force going to do in that six long months? … No one was paying them … They couldn't afford to stay around training and maintaining a state of readiness. I would estimate that by the time the Treaty was signed there was at least 30 per cent deterioration in our effectiveness and our structure and our morale. And this was a carefully calculated policy by the British.[2]

Although Barry's fear did in fact turn into reality, at the time of the announcement of the Truce, those men who had been on the run were able to return to their homes and their families. This was true for Seán, Robert and William Hales. But what were they going home to? During the war, their house had been burned down by the crown forces, which had a devastating effect on their father's health. Also, their farm help, John Murphy, had been shot dead by the British. Tom Hales later wrote:

On Sunday June 26, 1921, a column of the Essex Regiment arrested John Murphy, Cloghane, Ballinadee, Bandon, a young man in the prime of life, and a member of the Volunteer organisation. (His membership was not known to the enemy.) The enemy knew that he was employed as a worker on the farm for Seán Hales at Knocknacurra. Murphy was intercepted by this Essex Column, less than one mile to the west of Knocknacurra, on the Bandon road ... Around 2 o'clock ... the Essex Column arrived in the yard at Knocknacurra. Murphy was a prisoner with them then. They departed for Kilmacsimon taking Murphy with them. Around 10 o'clock next day, Patrick McCarthy, Kilmacsimon, reported to the IRA Section leader, Con Flynn, that he had made a terrible discovery in the lonely glen owned by him, less than a mile from Knocknacurra, adjoining the Kilmacsimon road. Flynn and local members of the IRA were on the scene to make a heart rending discovery. Examination revealed that Murphy had been butchered almost to death first ... then shot and thrown in over the fence on the left, where the cross to his memory now stands.[3]

Although those who had been on the run could now move about freely without fear of arrest or worse, those Volunteers in prison, including Tom Hales, were not going to be released any time soon. At best they would no longer be treated as common criminals but as political prisoners, but in prison they were to stay. However, while the Volunteers in the prisons in Ireland were granted prisoner-of-war status and could associate freely with their fellow comrades, those Volunteers in the prisons in England had to fight for that recognition. Tom Hales, in a newspaper interview shortly after his release from prison, told of what he and his comrades had to endure:

News of the truce came to them, and inducements were held out, but they held stubborn to the view that they should be treated as prisoners of war or as political prisoners. Mr. Hales went on to describe scenes within the prison, when more than one of his comrades was sent to the 'silent Cell' and the 'straight jacket', one of them refusing food for several days. He was eventually sent to hospital. The protest continued, every one of the prisoners refusing to don convict garb, until at last there was a 'food strike', at which the authorities became alarmed. Then came the IRA military order from within the prison for every man to hand out his coat and cap to each prison official commanding a landing. 'From that point ... every one of my comrades refused to wear prison uniform or to obey prison discipline.' He himself was examined by the Pentonville prison doctor. He was told he would be removed to Portsmouth. 'I was handcuffed … and told to put on prison clothes. I refused, and was then taken in an overcoat on the way to Portsmouth.'[4]

Back in Bandon, Seán and his brothers were readjusting to normal life. Seán gave public talks about the recent campaign. In a letter to his brother Donal in Italy, dated 2 October 1921, he wrote:

> If I had time at my disposal, I would very much like to give you a little history of that wonderful struggle or at least the first part of it, for it is too much to think that it is finished. No matter, on, on. Our dead did not die for anything short of Freedom, free from that Monster Empire under which we have suffered so long and so cruelly, the spirit of our people is good. The spirit of our Army [is] better, but, it is from the flames and the ashes that the star of liberty will rise.[5]

On 11 October 1921 talks between the Irish and British governments began in London with the aim of negotiating a treaty between the two countries. The Irish delegation consisted of Arthur Griffith, Michael Collins, Robert Barton, Éamon Duggan and George Gavan Duffy. For the next two months these men discussed and debated, in often heated exchanges, with a formidable British delegation.[6] During this time Collins managed to make contact with many of his comrades being held in the English prisons, including Tom Hales:

There was a tinge of sadness in his visits to his long-time friend and fellow west Cork man, Tom Hales in Pentonville. Despite being under surveillance, he did succeed, speaking some Irish, in conveying to Hales the difficulties of getting a Republic from the British. Hales was very special to him, it was a friendship that went very far back.[7]

In reality a Republic was never going to be granted; too much was at stake for the British Empire. Palestine, Egypt, India and other countries under British rule were watching, and in some cases taking inspiration from, Ireland. If Britain granted full independence to one of her colonies, then no doubt others would make the same demands. The empire had to be preserved at all costs.

Finally, in the early hours of 6 December 1921, under the threat of 'immediate and terrible war', the Anglo-Irish Treaty was signed by the Irish and British delegates. The Treaty, as we know, did not give full freedom to Ireland: instead, Ireland would now become a Free State, a dominion within the British Empire with some control over her own affairs. An Irish parliament would be established, and there would be an Irish army and police force. Partition, which had come into effect as part of the Government of Ireland Act in June 1920, was cemented and the country would consist of two states: the Free State in the southern part of the country; and in the province of Ulster, the six-county state of Northern

Ireland. But what proved to be most unpalatable for many Republicans was the fact that the Irish members of parliament had to swear an oath of allegiance to the British monarch. The Treaty was far from perfect, but to use Collins' words, it was a 'stepping-stone' to achieve full freedom. Under the terms of the Treaty, there was to be a general amnesty for all IRA prisoners and on 12 December 1921 Tom Hales, amongst many others, was unconditionally released from Portsmouth Prison.

Despite his newfound freedom, Tom did not return to Ireland immediately; there was one place he wished to visit before leaving England. He told a reporter for the *Irish Independent* that 'He had visited Broadmoor Lunatic Asylum, where he found 5 of the prisoners, who had been either in Pentonville, Portland, or Wormwood Scrubbs [*sic*], closely confined. Three of the five, he said, are hopeless lunatics.'[8] One of the men he visited was his friend Pat Harte, whose condition had deteriorated badly. Within three years Harte would be dead as a result of his treatment after his arrest and imprisonment.

When Collins and the Irish delegation returned to Ireland with the Treaty, it was immediately realised that this agreement was not satisfactory to all. Not only did the Treaty divide the country; it also divided the Republican movement, both the political and military factions. More sadly the Treaty divided families, including the Hales. They did not have time to celebrate the return of Tom; instead there was division, as both Seán and Madge supported the Treaty, while Tom, Robert and William rejected it.

For the next month there were many debates between the pro- and anti-Treaty factions in the Dáil on the Treaty. Both sides were adamant in their arguments; no one could be swayed. In the 1921 general election Seán Hales had been elected to represent the Cork Mid, North, South, South East and South West constituency, and in his position as TD he addressed the Dáil in support of the Treaty. His support was, it can be said, unexpected, when one considers what he and his family suffered between 1916 and 1921. Speaking at a private session of the Dáil, he stated:

There has been so much speaking over this extraordinary question that the only thing I have to say on it is from a military point of view. If I thought that this Treaty which was being signed was to bar our right to freedom, if it was to be the finality, I wouldn't touch it but I took it that it is to be a jumping off point to attain our alternative ends … The only thing is that at the present moment if there was anything like a split it would be more dangerous than anything else. As for our principle we are all pledged to that which is to place Ireland in her place amongst the nations of the earth … Posterity will judge us all yet … Speaking from the column which I was always with through the battlefields and willing and ready to carry on the fight but I still look upon that Treaty as the best rock from which to jump off for the final accomplishment of the Irish freedom. There is no doubt but speaking in these momentous times because it takes men of iron will to stand up against that question of principle because he would be apt to be misjudged. He might be called a coward. There is no cowardice in it but there is real commonsense in the South ... The only thing that I would like to be understood in is that any kind of division would have a terrible effect. As for the people on the whole they are for this Treaty and I don't care what sense they are for it because some vote for any peace ... There is hardly one of us here could realise what it is to have that army of occupation gone because in a short time with the building up of the youth of the country, the training of their minds and the training of them as soldiers and the equipping, that the day will soon be at hand when you could place Ireland to my mind in her rightful place amongst the nations of the earth. The feeling in the South amongst the ordinary people is surely for the Treaty, even the best of them were tired and war worn out. There is no getting away from it but still if they are called upon again they will give their help to the soldiers of Ireland. They gave what they had and they will give what is remaining but I consider and I have weighed it up and watched the whole proceedings. I don't speak with animosity to any man but I speak as a soldier because it is the soldiers who will win this fight, it is not the politicians ... We had a great precedent about keeping treaties with England ... when Sarsfield under duress signed the Treaty with the English King, he honourably kept his word and they honourably broke it. Well, the day is coming when we will pay that back ... Ireland's destiny is to be a Republic and the man who gets the closest and soonest to that in the best way is the man.[9]

In a public session of the debates he reiterated his feelings, stating:

I have travelled down this stormy road since 1916 and it is conviction that leads me to vote for this Treaty; I know my friends and fellow-soldiers on the other side are equally convinced; but I can find no other way out at the present moment ... some one might say that I had not the courage of my convictions, I now state publicly that I am going to vote for this Treaty.[10]

As the debates wore on, the tension between both sides was becoming more evident and, as a result, friendships began to deteriorate between men who had just a short time before fought together. Liam Deasy, adjutant of the Third West Cork Brigade, described the situation:

We had to listen to men who a few short months before were fighting as comrades side by side, now indulging in bitter recrimination, rancour, invective charges and counter charges. Gone was the old chivalry and *esprit de corps*.[11]

Finally a vote was taken on the issue of the Treaty. On 7 January 1922 it was ratified by sixty-four votes to fifty-seven. In response, Éamon de Valera resigned as president of Dáil Éireann, to be replaced by Arthur Griffith, and left the proceedings with his colleagues. Although this was a clear indication that there could be no agreement between the pro- and anti-Treaty factions, there was still hope that conflict between them could be avoided.

7

DIVISION

With the ratification of the Treaty, the British withdrawal from the twenty-six counties began. A Provisional Government was established and existed from when the Treaty was ratified until the official establishment of the Irish Free State, which would take place within a year. Richard Mulcahy, who had replaced Cathal Brugha as Minister for Defence, stated that 'the Army [IRA] will remain the Army of the Irish Republic'.[1] This was a noble statement but, as was the case with Dáil Éireann, the IRA was also split over the Treaty, with most of the brigades rejecting it. But despite their obvious differences, it was believed that an agreement could be reached to avoid a complete breakdown in relations.

To complicate matters, the situation as it stood was not as clear-cut as simply the IRA being split into pro- and anti-Treaty factions. Some members of the anti-Treaty IRA felt that by remaining under the Dáil's control they would have no say in the setting up of the new army, which was later to become the National Army. It was felt by them that it would be better if the army was removed from the control of the Dáil and reverted to its independent position.[2] To make their concerns known, they sent a letter to Mulcahy requesting that an Army Convention be held as soon as possible to discuss the army's position. Their proposals to Mulcahy were that they would reaffirm their allegiance to the Republic; an Executive would be set up to control the army; and they would have their own constitution. An independent headquarters would be established if this proposal was not accepted. However, these views were not held by many of the anti-Treaty officers, who still viewed the Dáil as the legitimate government of the Republic and did not agree initially to the removal of the army from its control.

Mulcahy and Michael Collins could not risk an all-out split in the army at this time, so on 18 January 1922 they met with anti-Treaty officers, including Liam Lynch and Ernie O'Malley, to discuss the situation. Mulcahy was adamant that the IRA should remain under the control of the Dáil. It was suggested by Mulcahy and Collins that the proposed Army Convention be held in March. Also, a council of four, a committee made up of pro- and anti-Treaty officers, would be set up to ensure that the IRA GHQ in Dublin, many of whose members supported the Treaty, would not do anything to undermine the Republic declared on Easter Monday 1916.

This compromise was not acceptable to all in the anti-Treaty faction, but Liam Lynch, O/C First Southern Division, anti-Treaty, did not approve of his anti-Treaty comrades' proposals to remove the army from the control of the Dáil, and his personality was such that he was able to persuade his comrades to follow his lead and oppose this suggestion, for a time at least. His division was after all the strongest, both numerically and in terms of men trained in battle. After much deliberation, and with some reluctance, the proposals put forward by Collins and Mulcahy were agreed to.

Beggars Bush Barracks was the first to be evacuated by the British. On 31 January 1922 it was formally handed over to pro-Treaty forces under the command of General Paddy O'Daly. It was decided by GHQ that an officer's training camp would be set up, and senior officers from all the IRA divisions, whether pro- or anti-Treaty, would be selected by their members to attend. Those officers would then return to their respective areas and set up similar camps and train their officers.[3]

Although it seemed that both sides were placated, the division grew deeper. As the British withdrew their forces, barracks were handed over to both pro- and anti-Treaty factions of the IRA. Unlike the rest of the country, where barracks were handed over to the local IRA regardless of their stance, in Dublin the British handed over the barracks only to the pro-Treaty faction. Then, at the end of February, events in Limerick threatened to erupt into civil war when the two sides refused to leave the city. The anti-Treaty IRA should have taken over the barracks in the city, as they were the local force, but the Provisional Government felt that Limerick was, strategically, too important a position to be in the hands of the anti-Treaty IRA and should be held by the pro-Treaty forces. Soldiers from the First Western Division, led by Michael Brennan, occupied various barracks in the city, while anti-Treaty IRA forces also occupied buildings, and tensions in the city soon reached breaking point. While Arthur Griffith and some other members of the Provisional Government wanted the pro-Treaty army to take the city, by force if necessary, cooler heads prevailed. Liam Lynch and Oscar Traynor from the anti-Treaty side met with Collins, Mulcahy and Eoin O'Duffy and, in an attempt to stave off the threat of civil war, it was eventually agreed that the pro-Treaty troops would withdraw from the city and Limerick Corporation would take over the majority of the evacuated barracks.[4]

Because of the Limerick crisis, the Army Convention was banned and it was announced that *any* officer who attended it would be suspended from the army. The ban was ignored by the anti-Treaty IRA and on 26 March 1922 over 200 delegates, representing fifty-two out of seventy-

three brigades, attended the convention. It was held in the
Mansion House, Dublin, where:

> The Delegates reaffirmed their allegiance to the Republic, de-
> nounced the Treaty, and elected an Executive of 16 in whom
> they vested supreme control of the army. The Executive repudi-
> ated the authority of the Minister for Defence [Mulcahy], and
> the Chief-of-Staff [Eoin O'Duffy] and most of significantly
> [*sic*], repudiated the authority of Dáil Éireann.[5]

Tom Hales and Liam Deasy, now adjutant of the First Southern Division, were elected to the Executive.[6] These appointments were to be temporary until a second convention could
be held. An election would then be called to elect a permanent Executive and a constitution would be drawn up.

In the meantime both sides set about putting their views
on the Treaty before the people and pro- and anti-Treaty
rallies were held all over the country. These meetings were,
more often than not, very heated gatherings, with supporters
from both sides trying to disrupt the proceedings. At one
pro-Treaty meeting at Grand Parade in Cork city in March,
both Michael Collins and Seán Hales were present. Thousands of people attended and before Seán Hales spoke a
number of shots were fired from the crowd. As one reporter
commented:

Mr Hales stood unperturbed … raising his voice, [he] addressed the interrupters. He said: 'The British Army did not frighten me. Those shots do not frighten me' … He stood for the Republic and would continue to stand for the Republic, but he stood on the only road along which that Republic could be gained … No power on earth will frighten me, declared Mr Hales, and [he] retorted with emphasis, 'We strove and fought for Irish freedom in 1916 and I had one aim and object in this life, and that was the freedom of our people. We did not strike to break one tyranny and plant another … If any man … has an argument or says I am a traitor, let him face me … I am one of those … who was in the fight from the start to the finish. I am one of those who know how Ireland stands at the present moment, and I was not one of those who asked for the truce.'

… No one … had greater or deeper regard for the courage of some of the men in the IRA who were now opposed to him. He knew well they were good men, but there had to be a choice of two roads … But they should not destroy the nation.

… The man who fired the first shot in an internecine war in Ireland would be guilty of the greatest crime against the country … The issue was not Free State or Republic, or if it were he knew where he would be. He fought as a soldier who loved his country, and would again if necessary.[7]

On 2 April Tom Hales spoke at an anti-Treaty meeting in his hometown of Bandon. Again, thousands of people gathered and Tom was warmly received by the crowd. Speaking on his position regarding the Treaty, he said:

It was the people sent them out to fight, and elected a government and gave it a mandate to govern the country. They thereby sent the men who had gone to their graves. Were they going to vote away that independence that they had sent them out to fight for and for which those men died ... There was no man he respected in the past more than Michael Collins. People asked how was it Michael Collins was wrong. He [Hales] believed that if he kept from Lloyd George and his intrigue he would have a republic today. It was also asked why he and his brother Seán differed. As an army officer he knew his brother's work and what he really did. They may ask why he voted for the treaty, and people asked how could they go wrong. Well, if the first people God made went wrong, it was likely enough that they should go wrong. If his brother stuck to the principles he held always he would be on their side today ... As Brig. Comdt. [*sic*] of this area, he said the republican army would continue, and he would do everything for peace and happiness and prosperity ... He was not a speechmaker, but he once more appealed for unity in the army. If war came, let it come, for though they talked of it as a horrible thing, it would be a grand thing.[8]

There it was, both brothers stating emphatically their reasons for accepting and rejecting the Treaty. Although neither would stray from their allegiance, neither would they be drawn to denigrate each other and, as can be seen, neither wanted civil war to become a reality. But if civil war did break out, both would be more than willing to fight for what they believed in.

J. J. Bradley, a member of the South-East Cork County

Council, of which Seán Hales was president and chairman, was unlucky enough to suffer Seán's wrath at a council meeting held in Ballinadee on 16 April. The meeting was called to assess how many members of the Sinn Féin clubs or branches accepted the Treaty:

> When routine business concluded the chairman [Seán Hales] warned all present on the occasion, that on no account was anyone to carry out reprisals or interfere with other meetings ... He then turned to me and asked what the position of the I.R.A. members were [*sic*] in my District, meaning were they pro- or anti-treaty. I replied that the Captain and two Lieutenants were 'Republican', and was proceeding, when his face became distorted with anguish and rage ... He interrupted me, and in a terrible voice shaking with emotion he asked me did I not think him as good a Republican as any. 'If I thought,' he said, 'that I had done an injury to the Republic by voting for the acceptance of the Treaty, I'd have cut that right hand of mine off,' raising his right hand in the air 'before I'd do such a thing' and he continued 'don't you ever make such a distinction again'.[9]

Seán was insulted that Bradley referred to the anti-Treaty members as Republican, which he then understood to mean that anyone who accepted the Treaty was not a Republican. Many who accepted the Treaty, including Seán, did so in order to achieve the Republic and were committed to attaining it by using the Treaty as a means to an end.

In Dublin, tension was mounting between the moderate and extreme factions of the anti-Treaty IRA. On 9 April the second Army Convention was held, once again in the Mansion House, and a permanent Executive was established. Those who had been elected to the temporary Executive at the first Convention retained their appointments. A new Republican Constitution was ratified, which stated that 'the army would retain the title of the Irish Republican Army and would continue to function as had the pre-truce IRA; that is, it would be on a Volunteer basis. Its aims were to uphold the independence of the Republic, to protect the rights of its citizens and to serve an established Republican government that was wholly loyal to the Republic and its people.'[10]

A motion was put forward that the forthcoming election on 16 June be proclaimed as an illegal act and everything should be done to prevent it from taking place.[11] This proposal was seen as too extreme by the moderates amongst the anti-Treaty IRA, including Tom Hales, Liam Lynch, Florrie O'Donoghue and Seán O'Hegarty, to name a few. These four were members of the Executive and although they had decided not to accept the Treaty, they felt it was not their right to deny the people a chance to voice their opinion and vote on the issue. They were, after all, meant to be the representatives of the people, and if the people chose to accept the Treaty, they had no right to disagree with them. The motion was put to a vote and was defeated. But this issue highlighted the differences of opinion between the anti-Treaty Executive and many of the anti-Treaty officers. Realising that their views were very different in relation to what policy should be adopted, Tom Hales, Florrie O'Donoghue and Seán O'Hegarty resigned their positions on the Executive. O'Hegarty, in a letter to Liam Mellows, made clear his feelings, which it can safely be said would be the same for both Hales and O'Donoghue regarding the matter. O'Hegarty wrote:

My attitude of direct conflict with the majority view of the Executive as evidenced by this afternoon's decision on policy makes it impossible for me to continue as member of the Executive and accordingly I hereby tender my resignation.[12]

Tom Barry, Tom Derrig and Pax Whelan replaced Hales, O'Donoghue and O'Hegarty on the Executive.

On 26 April events in West Cork overshadowed, for a time at least, the political drama that was unfolding. That night, Commandant Michael O'Neill of Kilbrittain led a party of Volunteers to the home of Thomas Hornibrook at Ballygroman House, Ovens. Hornibrook was a member of the Protestant community in West Cork and a staunch loyalist. The IRA, it has been said, was there to commandeer his car. O'Neill and his men gained entry into Hornibrook's residence after he failed to answer the door. Soon after entering, shots were fired from within the house by Herbert Woods, an ex-British Army officer and Hornibrook's son-in-law. O'Neill was mortally wounded and soon after his death, Thomas Hornibrook, his son Samuel and son-in-law Herbert Woods were taken from Ballygroman House and executed by the IRA. Their bodies were never recovered.

Over the next four nights, ten members of the Protestant community in the West Cork area were murdered. It has been suggested by some historians that these were deliberate sectarian killings, sanctioned by the local leadership of the anti-Treaty IRA.[13] However, this has been disputed in the recent publication *Massacre in West Cork: The Dunmanway and Ballygroman Killings*. Historian Barry Keane has proved that the killings and the reasons for them were much more complicated and confusing than the simple explanation offered by some.[14] In the course of my research I did not find any proof to support the suggestion that the killings were ordered or supported by the West Cork command – in fact I found the opposite. At the time of the killings, officers of the West Cork Brigade were in Dublin attending the Army Convention and were unaware of the events that were taking place. On hearing of what had happened, Tom Hales, together with Tom Barry, Flor Begley and Seán Buckley amongst others, immediately returned to Cork to assess the situation and set about organising patrols of men to guard the Protestant community. Jim Kearney, a member of the West Cork IRA, stated, 'the Third Brigade had a guard on the [loyalist] Protestant houses at that time to protect them. I was one of the guards so I should know.'[15]

Tom Hales went further. As O/C of the West Cork Brigade, he felt it was his duty to assert his control over his men. He wrote:

On Friday, April 28th, I issued a definite military order to all battalion commandants in this Brigade, for transmission to all men under their command, that any soldier in the area was neither to interfere with nor insult any person. If said order will not be rigidly adhered to by all units those concerned will be dealt with in a manner not alone upholding the rigid discipline of a military force, but, in justice to the glorious tradition of the officers and men of the Brigade, even capital punishment will be meted out if necessary.

In case of civilians, all such offenders will be vigorously hunted up, and handed over by us to the constituted tribunals acting under Dáil Éireann. I promise to give all citizens in this area, irrespective of creed or class, every protection within my power. In furtherance of an order already issued to the I.R.A. to hand in any arms in their possession, I now order all citizens holding arms without a permit to hand them into O/C barracks at Bandon, Clonakilty, Ballineen, Dunmanway or Kinsale.

Anybody found in possession of arms in this area after this date will be severely dealt with.

Tom Hales

Brigade Commandant.[16]

With the situation in West Cork under control, attention once again focused on the issue of the widening division in the Republican movement. Both sides still felt there was a chance to unite the army, and again the Hales brothers were there to do what they could.

8

ATTEMPTS AT UNITY

By April 1922 the situation in Dublin was becoming increasingly tense. Two armies calling themselves the IRA now existed in the capital and the threat of civil war was growing. This was not helped by the fact that in the early hours of Good Friday, 14 April, members of the anti-Treaty IRA took over the Four Courts, right in the heart of the city. The anti-Treaty leadership, most notably Rory O'Connor and Liam Mellows, who had originally set up their headquarters in the Gaelic League Hall at No. 44 Parnell Square, realised that their present headquarters was unsuitable for their needs and so decided to find a more suitable location.

The taking over of the Four Courts was a huge embarrassment to the Provisional Government. How could they stand by and let this action proceed? The Four Courts was a very significant structure and this was a very powerful, very symbolic act on the part of the anti-Treaty IRA. Moreover, they had taken over the building with ease.[1] Realising that this action could be perceived as a direct threat to the government, the IRA Executive was quick to point out that although they had seized the building, they were not trying to initiate conflict. They were simply in need of a more suitable headquarters. In a news conference on 15 April 1922, Rory O'Connor, speaking on behalf of the Executive, was adamant when he stated:

> The occupation of the building should not be taken in any way as a coup d'etat, nor did it indicate the beginning of a revolution … He said they wanted that place as the premises they had in Parnell Sq. were not sufficient to accommodate them.[2]

Arthur Griffith and his colleagues in the Provisional Government were forced to watch as events unfolded. Although they, the politicians, were eager to assert their authority, they needed the support of Michael Collins and his officers in the army, who, as of yet, were unwilling to act against those they still regarded as comrades.

Meanwhile, in the background, the military on both sides were still trying to reach a compromise. In their eyes, the situation had not deteriorated so much that an agreement could not be reached, which can be seen from the publication of the proposals for army unity on 1 May. This came about as a result of negotiations between pro- and anti-Treaty

IRA officers, who included, amongst others, Tom Hales and Michael Collins. The document read:

> We, the undersigned officers of the I.R.A., realising the gravity of the present situation in Ireland, and appreciating the fact that if the present drift is maintained a conflict of comrades is inevitable, declare that this would be the greatest calamity in Irish history, and would leave Ireland broken for generations.
>
> To avert this catastrophe we believe that a closing of the ranks all round is necessary.
>
> We suggest to all leaders, Army and political, and all citizens and soldiers of Ireland the advisability of a unification of forces on the basis of acceptance and utilization of our present national position in the best interests of Ireland; and we require that nothing shall be done which would prejudice our position or dissipate our strength.
>
> We feel that on this basis alone can the situation best be faced, viz:
>
> (1) The acceptance of the fact – admitted by all sides – that the majority of the people of Ireland are willing to accept the Treaty.
> (2) An agreed election with a view to
> (3) Forming a Government which will have the confidence of the whole country.
> (4) Army unification on above basis.
>
> Dan Breen   Tom Hales
> H. [Humphrey] Murphy   S. [Seán] O'Hegarty

F. [Florrie] O'Donoghue   Seán Boylan

R. J. [Richard] Mulcahy   Owen O'Duffy

Gearóid O'Sullivan   Mícheál Ó Coileain.[3]

Upon publication of the document, the IRA Executive in the Four Courts immediately denounced it.

What this document achieved, for a brief time at least, was to force the politicians into talks with each other to see if conflict could be averted. As a result, a Dáil Peace Committee was established, with five representatives from both sides. Headed by Kathleen Clarke, the anti-Treaty members included Harry Boland, Liam Mellows, Seán Moylan and P. J. Ruttledge. Representing the pro-Treaty side were Seán Hales, Seán MacEoin, Joseph McGuinness, Séamus O'Dwyer and Pádraig Ó Máille.[4] Sadly, their efforts proved fruitless and within three weeks the talks between them broke down.

Also as a result of the army unity document, a Joint Army Committee was set up on 4 May. Again there were ten members, five from each side. This time, however, unlike the anti-Treaty members who signed the army unity document, those representing the anti-Treaty IRA were *all* members of the Executive: Liam Lynch, Liam Mellows, Seán Moylan, Rory O'Connor and Séamus Robinson. Representing the pro-Treaty side were Michael Collins, Richard Mulcahy, Seán MacEoin, Eoin O'Duffy and Gearóid O'Sullivan.[5]

The committee agreed to call a truce between the pro- and anti-Treaty forces. The previous months had seen sporadic outbreaks of violence between the two sides throughout the country. More importantly, the Joint Army Committee's efforts to unite both factions led to the signing of the Collins–de Valera Pact on 20 May. Among the terms of the Pact it was agreed that:

> ... a coalition panel of pro- and anti-Treaty Sinn Féin candidates would be put before the people. Rather than voting on whether to accept or reject the Treaty, the people would instead be voting on who they preferred to see elected to the government. A coalition executive was to be established, including a Minister for Defence representing the army, along with nine other ministers from both sides: five from the majority party and four from the minority. If this coalition broke down, then a general election was to be held in which the people would decide whether to accept the Treaty or not.[6]

The Collins–de Valera Pact gave hope that unity could be achieved. Another Army Committee was soon set up, consisting of eight officers, to make sure the Provisional Government did not disestablish the Republic proclaimed in 1916 and again at the formation of the Dáil in 1921. Representing the pro-Treaty side were Richard Mulcahy, Seán McMahon, Eoin O'Duffy and Gearóid O'Sullivan. Liam Lynch, Seán

Moylan, Rory O'Connor and Ernie O'Malley represented the anti-Treaty side. With regards to the terms of the Pact, it was suggested by Mulcahy that an Army Council would be elected and as such would have the authority to approve the appointments of the Minister for Defence and the army's chief of staff, as nominated by the government. Over the next few days there was much toing and froing between the factions, but eventually agreement was reached, not only between Mulcahy and his officers on the pro-Treaty side and Liam Lynch and his moderates on the anti-Treaty side, but also with Rory O'Connor and his comrades on the anti-Treaty Executive. As a result of talks, the IRA Executive agreed on 26 May to evacuate the buildings they held throughout Dublin city, except the Four Courts and those being used to house refugees from Belfast.[7]

Despite their earlier concessions, in early June, after much negotiation, the Army Committee's proposal regarding the government nominating the Minister for Defence and chief of staff was rejected by the anti-Treaty IRA Executive. Division was again becoming evident between the moderates and extremists within the anti-Treaty IRA. The Executive then proclaimed that they believed the upcoming general election to be an illegal act by the government.

Not only was there division within the anti-Treaty IRA, but any hope that army unity could be achieved was completely lost when, a few days before the election, Michael Collins publicly repudiated the Pact and urged the people to vote in the forthcoming general election for the Treaty. However, it was unlikely that the Pact would have achieved its aim of uniting the opposing sides anyway. The Free State Constitution, which was the one thing the anti-Treaty faction believed would be in their favour, was published on the morning of 16 June, the day of the election. As it was written mainly by members of the IRB, they believed it would do everything to uphold the Republic, but in this they would be disappointed. Instead, the Constitution reflected the agreements made by the Anglo-Irish Treaty, with the most unpalatable part being that every member of Dáil Éireann must swear an oath of allegiance to the British monarch.

The results of the election spoke loud and clear: the people were in favour of the Treaty. The hope of a coalition government was gone. Pro-Treaty Sinn Féin won fifty-eight seats, non-Sinn Féin candidates who were pro-Treaty won thirty-four seats and anti-Treaty Sinn Féin won just thirty-six seats in total.[8] The threat of civil war was now, more than ever, becoming a terrible reality.

For those on the anti-Treaty side, especially the Executive, they could not and would not accept the results of the election. The oath of allegiance to a foreign King was, for many, a betrayal too far. They feared that the new government would no longer fulfil the democratic programme of the first Dáil and secure an Irish Republic, the Republic which they had fought for. On the other side, the Provisional Government, which now had a mandate from the people, would have to act against the anti-Treaty forces.

It was now a matter of waiting to see who would strike first. And despite their efforts, both Tom and Seán Hales were unable to stop what looked like the inevitable from happening. In the coming months they would have to choose between their beliefs and their relationship.

9

THIRD ARMY CONVENTION
AND CIVIL WAR

Because of the favourable results of the general election, pressure was now put on the Provisional Government to act against the anti-Treaty forces. The British, eager to see the Treaty upheld, wanted the new government to stand firm and assert its authority. The Irish people had declared their support for the Treaty and if the Provisional Government was unwilling to take control of the country, then they, the British, were capable and willing to do so instead. The Provisional Government could not allow this to happen, but while the politicians were eager to make a stand against the anti-Treaty forces, the military were still unwilling to move against their former comrades.

Events took place on 18 June 1922 that could make it possible for the Provisional Government to act without actually causing a full-scale conflict. On that day the third Army Convention was held in the Mansion House. Liam Lynch, chief of staff of the anti-Treaty IRA, tried to put before the delegates the army unity proposals, even though they had been rejected already by the Executive. He believed that all the delegates should be given a chance to decide if they would accept or reject the proposals. However, the topic of debate was soon changed when Tom Barry suggested that, rather than discuss the issue of army unification, they should consider resuming hostilities against Britain. He put forward a proposal that the remaining British forces in Ireland, which were now only in Dublin and the six north-eastern counties, should be attacked if they failed to leave Ireland within seventy-two hours. This he felt would reunite the army, as he believed that the pro-Treaty forces would be more willing to fight the common enemy, Britain, than former comrades.[1]

A vote was taken and at first it looked like Barry's proposal had passed. A second count was demanded and the results showed that Barry's motion was defeated by 118 votes to 103. Because of the result, the defeated delegates, including most of the Executive, left the convention and returned to the Four Courts. Liam Lynch was deposed as chief of staff and Joseph McKelvey was appointed in his place. Lynch and his supporters, mostly from the First Southern Division of the IRA, made their way to the Clarence Hotel and set up a headquarters there. The anti-Treaty IRA was now split. This action by the Executive is hard to understand as, by deposing

Lynch as their chief of staff, they were cutting themselves off from the support of their comrades in the First Southern Division, which was at the time the largest division of the anti-Treaty IRA, comprising twelve brigades from counties Cork, Kerry, Waterford and west Limerick. Not only was this division strong in numbers, it was also one of the most, if not *the* most, experienced divisions with regard to men who had fought during the War of Independence.

Although this was disastrous for the anti-Treaty forces, the Provisional Government saw an opportunity. If Liam Lynch and his supporters could be kept out of the conflict, then the government could strike swiftly against the forces housed in the Four Courts, thus isolating the conflict in Dublin and ending it quickly.

Further pressure to act was put on the government when, on 22 June 1922, Sir Henry Wilson, military advisor to the six-county government, was shot dead in London by two IRA men, Reginald Dunne and Joseph O'Sullivan. Immediately the Executive forces in the Four Courts were blamed for the assassination and the British government demanded action from Arthur Griffith and his government.[2]

Plans were put in place by the British to attack the Four Courts if the Provisional Government failed to do so, but, re-alising that this would quite possibly reunite the IRA, they did not follow through with the plan. Instead, an ultimatum

Brigadier General Seán Hales (centre) discussing tactics with other members of the National Army, possibly in Kinsale, July/August 1922.
Courtesy of the Hales family

Wedding photograph of Tom Hales and Anne Lehane, 1928.
Courtesy of the Hales family

Robert Hales senior.
Courtesy of the Hales family

Donal Hales, Republican Envoy
in Genoa, Italy.
Courtesy of the Hales family

Madge Hales.
Courtesy of the Hales family

A joint RIC and Essex Regiment cycle patrol in West Cork during the War of Independence. *Courtesy of Mercier Archive*

Seán Hales' Luger. *Author's collection*

Above: The picture taken of Tom Hales and Pat Harte during their interrogation in July 1920.

Left: Captain Campbell Joseph O'Connor Kelly, one of the British officers identified by Tom Hales who engaged in his interrogation and subsequent torture after his arrest in July 1920. *Courtesy of Military Archives, BMH_CD_227_35*

British troops lower the Union flag during the handover of Victoria Barracks, Cork, to Irish forces in 1922. *Courtesy of Mercier Archive*

Michael Collins leaving the Munster Arms Hotel, Bandon, 22 August 1922. This photograph was taken just a few hours before his death. *Courtesy of Military Archives, PC 331*

The funeral procession of Seán Hales, Cork city, December 1922.
Courtesy of Military Archives

Members of the Third West Cork Brigade at the site of the Kilmichael ambush *c.* 1960s. *Front row* (left to right): Fr O'Brien, unidentified, Tom Barry, Tom Hales, Mossie Donegan. *Back row* (left to right): unidentified, Jim Barry, William Hales, unidentified. *Courtesy of the Hales family*

The memorial to Seán Hales, in Seán Hales Place, Bandon. *Author's collection*

IRA veterans at the unveiling of the memorial to Michael Collins in Sam's Cross in 1965. It includes members of 'The Squad' and officers of the Third West Cork Brigade. *Kneeling* (left to right): Tom Hales, Vinny Byrne, Joe McGuinness. Among those standing are Liam Deasy, Tom Barry (6th from left) and Paddy Lawson.
Courtesy of Military Archives, PC 253

Tom Hales *c.* 1965.
Courtesy of the Hales family

The funeral of Tom Hales, Bandon, 1 May 1966.
Courtesy of the Hales family

was sent to the Provisional Government to act, and act quickly. Collins was still not to be pushed and refused to do so. However, on 26 June an event took place that meant he could no longer ignore the situation. That night General J. J. 'Ginger' O'Connell of the pro-Treaty forces was kidnapped by members of the Four Courts garrison in retaliation for the arrest of one of their men, Leo Henderson. O'Connell was taken to the Four Courts, and the Executive demanded that Henderson be released in exchange for him. Their demand was ignored. Instead, the Provisional Government and, more importantly, Michael Collins finally decided to take action and at 4.10 a.m. on 28 June 1922, after requests to surrender their position and arms were ignored, pro-Treaty forces began to bombard the Four Courts with heavy artillery. The Civil War had begun.

Unfortunately for the Provisional Government, they did not have all the facts before them when they decided to attack the Four Courts. They believed that it was only the Dublin contingent of the IRA that they would have to deal with. Unbeknownst to them, however, earlier in the week Liam Lynch and his supporters had met with the IRA Executive in the Four Courts. After much discussion the two sides were able to put aside their differences in the hope that they could still unite the army and Lynch was reinstated as chief of staff of the anti-Treaty IRA. In fact Lynch had only left the Four Courts a few hours before it was attacked.

Lynch and his men agreed that they would stand by their comrades in Dublin. It was decided that he and his officers would return to their command areas in the south and mobilise their men for action. On leaving the Clarence Hotel, Lynch, together with Seán Culhane and Liam Deasy, made their way towards Kingsbridge (Heuston) Station. The three men were arrested by pro-Treaty forces and taken under guard to Wellington (Griffith) Barracks and held for a short time. While there, they were interviewed by Eoin O'Duffy. As the pro-Treaty forces were unaware of the change in circumstances within the anti-Treaty IRA, on the orders of Richard Mulcahy the three men were allowed to resume their journey back to Cork. The Provisional Government had let their single biggest threat walk away, and any hope of a swift end to the Civil War quickly vanished with the release of Liam Lynch.[3]

On 29 June a brigade meeting of anti-Treaty officers was held in Mallow Barracks with all brigade commanding officers present, including Tom Hales, O/C Third West Cork Brigade. Liam Deasy, who was present at the meeting, stated:

> Only one motion was put to this brief meeting. Only one decision was taken. That was a unanimous intent to organise our forces on a war footing, and to first capture Limerick city and so gain control of the Shannon crossing.[4]

The fighting in Dublin lasted eight days. The Four Courts garrison surrendered on 30 June, after which the fighting moved to O'Connell Street, where Oscar Traynor, O/C Dublin Brigade, and his men held out for five more days. By that time Dublin city centre once again lay in ruins. There were, of course, casualties on both sides, most notably Cathal Brugha, who was mortally wounded by pro-Treaty forces while trying to escape from the Granville Hotel on O'Connell Street, the last stronghold of the anti-Treaty forces. With Dublin city now predominantly controlled by the pro-Treaty forces, attention focused on the south and what was to become known as the 'Munster Republic'.

The inevitable had happened, and with Tom, William, Robert and Donal on the anti-Treaty side, and Seán and Madge firmly entrenched on the pro-Treaty side, all the Hales family could hope for was that somehow they would all emerge from the conflict unscathed.

10

BROTHERS AT WAR

The Third West Cork Brigade, like most of the pre-Truce IRA, rejected the Treaty. For most, the decision was clear-cut; their loyalty was to the Irish Republic declared in 1916, not the compromise of the Treaty. That decision was not to be so easy for the members of the Ballinadee Company, Third West Cork Brigade, as not only were they forced to decide whether or not to accept the Treaty, but they also had to choose which of their commanding officers they were loyal to: Seán or Tom Hales?

Tom Hales had been their commanding officer on the formation of the Ballinadee Company. Then, upon his promotion to O/C Bandon Battalion and later O/C Third West Cork Brigade, Seán had taken his place as commanding officer. The members had fought side by side with both brothers. They had served under them, had taken part in many successful engagements and had survived many encounters together. More sadly, they were their neighbours, childhood friends; theirs was a long and shared history. For the Ballinadee Company the only decision they could make was to remove themselves from the impending conflict. Rather than make an impossible choice, the company resigned *en masse*.

Tom Hales did try to persuade his comrades to join him, but he was only partly successful. In an unsigned letter to the O/C Organisation, First Southern Division IRA, in August 1922, on the reorganisation of the Third West Cork Brigade, it was stated that:

> I find the Organisation here far superior to Cork No. 5. The men who have fallen away are either Truce Volunteers, or men who were never active. The Adjt. has told me that only three men from the Brigade went to Beggars Bush [i.e. pro-Treaty], and that none of the men who have fallen away are inclined to take up arms on the other side. The Ballinadee Company resigned altogether, but the Brigade O/C [Tom Hales] has advised us to leave the matter in his hands and that he will be able to get them right again. Already 10 men have come over. This being his native place, I think it is best to do so.[1]

For those who took the pro-Treaty side, it was no longer safe to go as freely about their business as they had done since the Truce was called, especially in their home county. John L. O'Sullivan, who, like Seán Hales, was one of the few Cork men who took the pro-Treaty side and who fought under Seán's command in the Civil War, recalled:

> Feelings ran very high here in Cork and when the split appeared
> in the IRA it got bigger and deeper as time went on ... A lot of
> us here who were in favour of the Treaty had to go on the run,
> because the general body of the Volunteers around Cork were
> anti-Treaty, and they had taken over barracks and given us a
> pretty rough time ...[2]

With Dublin under the control of the pro-Treaty forces, and with Liam Lynch having established his command in Munster, the new National Army was forced to follow the conflict southwards. They wanted it to be over quickly and with as few losses as possible. However, the anti-Treaty forces had, as part of their policy, destroyed roads and railways all over the country to impede the National Army's advance. Moreover, travelling by road and rail would leave the National Army open to ambush, so instead they transported their men and equipment by boat and made a series of landings on the southern coast. Seán Hales, now a Brigadier General in the National Army, was on one such transport boat and on landing in Bantry he took command, moved his men to Skibbereen, and took the town successfully. Tom Hales and his men had been holding Skibbereen, but with the arrival of the National Army in large numbers it was decided to leave the town and keep on the move.

John L. O'Sullivan, formerly captain of 'L' Company, Second Battalion, Third West Cork Brigade, and a veteran of the War of Independence, was now a captain in the National Army and a close friend of Seán's. Recalling those early days of the Civil War in Cork, he stated:

> [Seán] Hales was a truly great man … We left Skibbereen on foot, and I remember he marched with me at the head of the column as we went to Clonakilty. We took Clonakilty and marched on to Courtmacsherry, and from a boat there we got in an 18-pound gun and four gunners and a Lancia armoured car and we hit off straight for Bandon. The other side had us under observation all day and they brought all their forces between Bandon and us.[3]

As the army tried to make their advance into Bandon, they came under increasing fire from the Republicans. Every time they tried to push forward, they were forced back by their unseen enemy. Seán Hales, in order to press ahead, called for the 18-pound gun to be used. But he was not about to unleash the full capability of the artillery on his former comrades or quite possibly his own brother. More than anything, it was to be a show of force. O'Sullivan continued the story:

> 'Now do you see that wood? That's our target,' he said … 'Now load the blank shell.' And someone said, 'Are you mad? A blank shell?' 'I'm not mad,' he said. 'A blank shell will do. I don't want to kill any of the poor devils.' They're the words he used … So

the blank shell was fired ... and it had the desired effect on the others because they retreated.[4]

This reluctance to kill, to be ruthless in the way that they had been against the British in the War of Independence, could be seen on both sides. As it stood, all was not lost; maybe an agreement could still be reached to end the fighting. Despite the fact that the Republicans held the advantage in terms of experienced, battle-hardened men – most of the anti-Treaty IRA were veterans of the War of Independence – they were more reluctant to put up a determined fight. In comparison, the National Army, as a result of the recruitment drives in early July, now numbered over 20,000 men, but most of these recruits had not fought in either the Easter Rising or the War of Independence, and obviously did not have the same relationship with each other as those who had fought together in the preceding years.

The Republicans' unwillingness to seize the initiative was to have detrimental effects on their campaign, as Liam Deasy noted:

They [National Army] had taken us by surprise when they began landing troops at strategic points on the coast ... The solid south, in which we had so much confidence, was completely broken ... Unfortunately we were forced to realise that things were not the same … The people were no longer enthusiastically with us as in the earlier fight … The second factor was the reluctance of so many Volunteers to face up to the harsh realities. They seemed to have no heart in the fight and the knowledge that they were fighting against their kith and kin, even brother against brother, must have also influenced them very much.[5]

John L. O'Sullivan, discussing Seán Hales' methods during the campaign, summed it up when he stated:

He had no wish to annihilate anybody; he was a man of peace. He was only doing the job he was put to do, and he wanted to do it with the least loss of life on both sides. He never stopped, he kept us on the move from the time we started until we took over every town and every village and every stronghold of the others in the area. But all the time you could see he was a man of peace.[6]

Official National Army records for this particular period in the Civil War regarding operations and strategy do not exist, as they only began to keep comprehensive records in late August 1922. However, testimonies do exist from some members of the National Army detailing events, like those of John L. O'Sullivan. Unlike the National Army, the Republicans did write reports and their records do exist for this period. So through Tom Hales' reports and O'Sullivan's accounts it is possible to piece together many of the events that took place in West Cork at this time.

Throughout the month of July Tom Hales was in regular contact with Liam Lynch, chief of staff of the anti-Treaty IRA, regarding his position and that of his brother. At this time he was faced with the difficulty of not just how to hold back the National Army's advance in West Cork, but also of how to keep his men organised. In one letter on 6 July he wrote:

> You must also remember the brigade is already taxed very heavy and in the face of … other circumstances there would be a danger of the organisation on the whole weakening …
>
> I also need not impress upon you that the main key to success is organisation … it was England's game in the past to burst our organisation, it is also Collins and Co's only hope of success.
>
> No individual effort counts when organisation is gone. Anyhow I will do my best in the matter.[7]

In a number of reports, between 13 and 26 July, he detailed how the National Army was continuing their advance. They needed to take control of Kinsale, a key position – a fact that Tom Hales was keenly aware of. In his report of 13 July he stated:

Two battleships are reported to be hovering round Kinsale harbour.

Whatever you think of this I personally think attention should be given to Kinsale.

... I am travelling to Kinsal[e] and over the whole coastal area and will report to you again my opinion as to the best that can be done under present circumstances.[8]

National Army activity continued around not only Kinsale, but also Garretstown, Howe Strand and other coastal areas. Tom Hales set up observation points from which he could monitor their movements, 'with a party of four rifle men at each, also bikes with daily communication with each other and with HQ'.[9] So it continued throughout July and August: Seán Hales and his forces pressing ahead while his brother and his men watched their movements.

As Kinsale was a key position that the National Army needed to take, eventually, by mid-August, the anticipated battle for the town took place between the opposing forces. Again, there are no official accounts of the events from the pro-Treaty side, but John L. O'Sullivan, who participated in the attack, recalled what happened:

After we took Bandon we went on for Kinsale. They had a bridge blown up there ... and we had no way of getting in except by boat. We had maybe a mile of river and bay to get across and

[Seán] Hales said to me, 'Crowd into the boats,' he said, 'and get across and try to capture the bridgehead on the other side.' So in we got and when we were halfway across they opened fire on us from the top of the hill. And they riddled the bloody place. The fellow sitting beside me got six holes from one bullet ... When the firing started the three fellows who were rowing ... they ducked down and let go of the oars and we were sitting ducks. The bullets were coming around us in the water ... and they were hitting the boat, taking chips off it ... two of us grabbed two oars and pulled, and we hadn't gone two lengths of the boat before we were as safe as we are sitting here now, because their line of fire was obscured once we got under the hill ... So anyway we took Kinsale and headed back for Bandon.[10]

Tom Hales received an account of the battle and forwarded a report to Liam Lynch. The 5th Battalion, Third Cork Brigade, was involved in this operation and Hales' account reiterates the statement made by John L. O'Sullivan:

O/C 5th had good engagement around Kinsal[e] union, reinforcements come from Kinsal[e] our side retired after 30 mins. Some coffins have come across dock w[h]ich shows their loss, some wounded also. Our side all well. Effective sniping in Bandon, on Tuesday evening and night. Enemy kept up firing all night.[11]

The National Army advance was complete by mid-August, with all the major towns in West Cork under their control.

The Republicans retreated but did not surrender and the war continued. The fear now was that, facing such well-armed opponents, the Republicans would revert to the tactics which had served them so well in the War of Independence: guerrilla warfare. A pro-Treaty report on 22 August stated:

> Our forces have captured towns, but they have not captured Irregulars and arms on anything like a large scale, and, until this is done, the Irregulars will be capable of guerrilla warfare … Our present dispositions leave us particularly exposed to guerrilla warfare … Our forces are scattered all over Command area … It is easy to isolate our posts.[12]

This fear was well founded as this is exactly what happened when the Republicans retreated to familiar territory: the hills and mountainous regions.

The Civil War was now entering its second phase. The time for staged battles was over. Just as before, both Seán and Tom Hales were again to play their part, only now the events that they were involved in were to bring the savagery of the Civil War to another, more tragic level.

11

THE DEATH OF COLLINS

The month of August 1922 would bring with it events that dramatically altered the course of the Civil War, and not for the better. With the pro-Treaty campaign in full swing, Michael Collins decided to make a tour of inspection around the southern counties to see for himself the progress being made by his troops. He left Dublin on 11 August, but his journey was abruptly cut short due to the sudden death of Arthur Griffith in Dublin on 12 August.[1] Collins returned to Dublin and attended Griffith's funeral on 16 August. He renewed his inspection tour on the morning of 20 August when he, together with an escort of fifteen men, including three officers, left Dublin.

Collins, it has been said, was undertaking this journey not just to see how the military campaign was progressing, but more importantly to see if there was a possibility of ending the Civil War in a way that would make it possible for both sides to retain some dignity. He was determined to pursue the war to the very end if necessary; however, his personal writings at the time suggest that this was not an option he favoured. He still respected his former comrades and he wrote that 'they should be given an opportunity of "Going home without their arms", provided they accepted "the People's verdict".' He stressed: 'We don't ask for any surrender of their principles' and concluded, 'We want to avoid any possible unnecessary destruction and loss of life' and 'We do not want to mitigate their weakness by resolute action beyond what is required'.[2]

Collins' eagerness to end hostilities was well known, as he was not in any way secretive in his actions. On his first inspection tour, just before Griffith's death, Collins visited Maryborough (Portlaoise) Prison, where he met Tomás Ó Maoileóin, anti-Treaty IRA, who had been arrested in July in Tipperary.[3] Ó Maoileóin, recalling the meeting, later wrote:

> I was transferred to Maryborough Prison. Within two weeks I had an unexpected visitor, Michael Collins. He was on his way south on the trip that preceded the funeral of Griffith in Dublin. He asked me would I attend a meeting of senior officers to try to put an end to this damned thing. He made arrangements with the Governor of the jail that I was to be released. As he went out, he slapped one fist into a palm in characteristic fashion: That's fine, the three Toms will fix it.

The three Toms mentioned by him were Tom Barry, Tom

Hales and myself. We were to meet in Cork with some of his officers and arrange for a cessation of hostilities.[4]

While Collins was preparing to meet some members of the anti-Treaty leadership, the Republicans were organising a meeting of their own officers, to take place on 22 August in West Cork. A meeting of the First and Third Cork Brigades had been held on 20 August in Ballyvourney, at which Liam Lynch expressed his wish to continue the campaign. Tom Hales was present and he disclosed his disapproval of Lynch's policy.

The meeting planned for 22 August was to be held in Bill Murray's house near Béal na mBláth, right in the heart of Republican territory. It was to be attended by officers of the five West Cork battalions and of the First Southern Division, which included Tom Hales and Liam Deasy. Amongst other things, they were there to discuss their present position and the possibility of ending the conflict.

Éamon de Valera was also in West Cork at this time. He had previously met Liam Lynch at his headquarters in Glanworth, Fermoy, where he urged Lynch to end the war. Lynch refused his request, after which de Valera made his way to West Cork where he was to contact Liam Deasy. De Valera arrived on the evening of 21 August and he and Deasy discussed the present situation at length.

In the meantime Michael Collins and his escort arrived in Cork. They had travelled through Tipperary, Limerick, Mallow and finally reached Cork city on the night of 20 August, where Collins met General Emmet Dalton at the Imperial Hotel, headquarters of the pro-Treaty forces in the city. The next day Collins inspected the various pro-Treaty positions around Cork city and then went to Macroom, where he met with Florrie O'Donoghue. O'Donoghue was one of many senior IRA men who refused to take part in the Civil War and instead opted to remain neutral.[5] Collins gave him a safe-conduct pass, as it was believed that through O'Donoghue and other neutral IRA officers a meeting with the Republicans could be arranged.

On the morning of 22 August Collins, with an escort of twenty-one men, left the Imperial Hotel to inspect the National Army strongholds throughout West Cork. The convoy 'consisted of a motor-cycle scout, Lieutenant Smith, an open Crossley tender with two officers, two Lewis-gunners, eight men armed with rifles, a touring car with Collins, Emmet Dalton and two drivers, Corry and Quinn, and finally an armoured car with revolving turret and Vickers machine-gun. A normal crew of four manned this armoured car.'[6]

The route they travelled was first to Macroom, then Bandon, Clonakilty and Skibbereen, finally returning to

Cork via Bandon that evening. The convoy reached Macroom and left there around 8 a.m. to proceed to Bandon. On the way the convoy stopped at Béal na mBláth to ask directions. Unknown to Collins and his escort, the person they asked was local IRA man Denny Long, who had been on scout duty throughout the night, keeping watch for National Army activity. With so many prominent Republicans in the area, it was necessary to have scouts keeping watch in case of possible raids by the National Army. Long told the convoy what direction to go in but was also quick to alert the Republicans as to who was in the locality.

Liam Deasy, who was arranging for de Valera to leave the area, as he (de Valera) was to return to Glanworth to meet with Liam Lynch, recalled:

I conveyed de Valera to Béalnabláth [*sic*] Cross ... We arrived there around 9.30 a.m. ... At the cross we were stopped by Denny Long who had been on scout duty during the night ... He told us a short time previously a Free State armed convoy consisting of a motor cyclist, a lorry of troops, a touring car and an armoured car had stopped to enquire the way to Bandon. Denny said he was most helpful to them as he was anxious to see them on their way quickly because of the Officers billeted in the nearby pub. He also told us that he recognised Michael Collins in the touring car. This was confirmed by Jerh [Jeremiah] Long who saw the convoy from his shop window.[7]

When de Valera enquired as to what was most likely to happen, Deasy explained to him, in no uncertain terms, that an ambush would be planned. According to Deasy, this troubled de Valera. Both he and Deasy proceeded to Bill Murray's, which was a short distance from Béal na mBláth. On arrival they found some of the Republican officers had already gathered and were discussing what action to take. Amongst them was Tom Hales. Bill Powell, who was in Murray's at the time, recalled:

> There was no great debate, the question was, should an ambush be prepared or not? There was disagreement about this. Tom Hales was cool and thoughtful ... He suggested that on balance they shouldn't ambush the returning convoy ... However, when all views were expressed, it was finally decided that the convoy was part of an enemy force encroaching on territory which the Republicans still held and that therefore it should be ambushed.[8]

Command of the operation was given to Tom Hales, who reluctantly organised his men and proceeded to plan the ambush. The scheduled meeting was to be delayed and the men dispersed. De Valera left for Glanworth before any definite plans were put in place.

Meanwhile, Collins and his convoy continued on their journey via Bandon to Clonakilty, Rosscarbery and Skibbereen. Having met with the various officers in each town Collins and his party left Skibbereen for their return journey back to Cork at around 4.30 p.m. Collins wished to visit his family home at Sam's Cross, where he met his brother Seán. After some time the convoy continued its journey but they had to return to Bandon before going back to Cork as he had arranged to meet with Seán Hales, who was in command of the garrison stationed there.[9] Hales ordered John L. O'Sullivan, Collins' cousin Maurice and a party of soldiers to go to Lee's Hotel, now the Munster Arms Hotel, and await Collins' arrival. Hales, who was in the Devonshire Arms Hotel, the barrack quarters, would follow on and meet them, as he had to prepare plans for their next operation, which was to take the town of Dunmanway.

When O'Sullivan and his men arrived at the hotel, they discovered Collins was already there. After a time the men were called in to see Collins, who enquired about their activities in the area. Collins was quite happy with their progress and 'when Seán Hales arrived, he was warmly greeted and congratulated by his superior officer and friend'.[10]

Collins and Hales discussed matters privately. Apparently Seán had been instrumental in organising the meeting between the neutral IRA men and Collins and, according to some, that meeting was to take place in Cork city that night.[11] They talked a little more about the situation and Hales alerted Collins to the fact that many of the roads were impassable due to the road blocks set up by the Republicans. He warned Collins that the route the latter would take to return to Cork would be dangerous, but his advice went unheeded. Collins left Hales and his men in good spirits and his parting words to them were, 'Keep up the good work. 'Twill soon be over.'[12]

Hales and his men watched as the convoy left Bandon. It would have to go through Crookstown and travel once more to Macroom before finally returning to Cork. This was the last time these men would see their commander-in-chief alive. Soon afterwards Seán Hales led his men out of Bandon, unaware of the disastrous events that were about to unfold and the pivotal role his younger brother Tom was to have in them.

As Collins continued his inspection tour, Tom Hales and a party of approximately twenty-five men lay in wait at Béal na mBláth. The location chosen for the ambush was ideal as the 'bóithrín meandered in an extended horseshoe overlooking the main road. In between was a marshy field, with bushes and ferns and a winding stream running parallel to the main road. Off this bóithrín were two smaller bóithríns running to other roads further north … This all meant that ready-made places of retreat were there.'[13]

Liam Deasy was not present at the ambush site for most of the day, as he had other matters to deal with, mostly administration work. Tom Hales ordered that a mine be laid on the road and that a roadblock should be constructed, which consisted of a horse-drawn cart commandeered by the Republicans. The cart was placed on a bend in the road, in a blind spot to the oncoming convoy, so it would take them completely by surprise. Hales positioned his men on the western side of the road behind a low fence. They were armed with revolvers, Lee Enfield rifles and Thompson submachine-guns. With everything in place, the men waited.

However, as the day wore on into the evening, and with no sign of Collins' convoy approaching, it was believed that they would not return via Béal na mBláth and that they must have travelled some other way. It was now past seven o'clock and Deasy, who had completed his duties, went to the ambush site to assess the situation. He recalled:

Jerh Long told us that the column was in ambush position and I walked down the Bandon road in that direction. There I met Tom Hales who was standing in the middle of the road. He told me that as the men had been in such an uncomfortable position all day, and as the convoy was not likely to return this way, he was giving an order to withdraw. He also ordered the Battalion Engineer to remove the mine and detailed four members of the column to remain in position as a protective party while this was being done.[14]

There are discrepancies as to where exactly Tom Hales was, following his decision to call off the ambush. According to

Liam Deasy, Hales, with Deasy and a number of others, made their way to Long's public house and were there about ten minutes when they heard the opening shots of the ambush.[15] However, according to Tom Kelleher, it was Hales, Jim Hurley and himself who decided to remove the cart from the road. After they had removed the roadblock, the three men split up; Kelleher and Hurley began to make their way to a local house, while Hales remained at the barricade. Soon they heard the advancing convoy.

The motor-cycle driver Smith, who was leading the convoy, on seeing the cable for the mine, immediately turned around, drove back to the Crossley tender, and alerted the troops as to what was happening. Emmet Dalton, who was in the touring car with Collins, instructed the driver to speed on ahead, but Collins countermanded his order and demanded they stop and fight. A gun battle developed between the Free State party and Republicans (presumably the protective party left behind to cover Hales and co.), with the soldiers from the tender taking up position on the road. But with very little cover, they were open targets.

Immediately the sound of gunfire could be heard throughout the vicinity. At the same time a party of IRA men, including John Lordan, captain of the Newcestown Company, and Bill Powell, captain of the First Cork Brigade, were walking along the road towards Béal na mBláth. On hearing the gunfire Lordan, Powell and their comrades leapt over a fence to take cover. They climbed a hill nearby, which overlooked Collins' convoy, and opened fire on the Crossley tender.

Meanwhile Tom Kelleher, believing that Hales would be caught in the crossfire, called to Jim Hurley to open fire on the convoy:

> 'Hales is at the barricade, he'll be destroyed,' shouted Kelleher. With speed the two men ran over the northern (lower) little bridge, wheeled around and fired a few shots into the air. Hales leaped when he heard the vehicles in the distance and ran to catch up with Bill Powell and John Lordan ... Any second they could be mowed down. The two men ran, leaped over the little ditch and began to grope the steep incline of furze and bushes. Hales followed almost immediately.[16]

The Republicans were not in full strength because of the order to withdraw and were spread out over a good distance. Kelleher and Hurley quickly returned to the ambush position:

> Tom Kelleher and Jim Hurley ... ran forward and headed further up the lower end (northern side) of the horseshoe bóithrín which was beyond where the barricade was located. They took up positions on the height. Hales, running to catch up with Powell and Lordan, jumped in beside the ditch at the eastern side, and vaulted over a low fence. Eventually he caught up with Bill Powell and John Lordan further up the furzy incline.[17]

Three other men took up position on the southern end of the bóithrín.

Collins' convoy was well armed with Thompson guns, rifles and of course the Vickers gun on the armoured car, which was manned by Jock McPeake. When the armoured car came to a halt, McPeake opened fire on the surrounding area. After a time he ran into difficulty and the gun seized up. Collins, at this time, was further north up the road and at every chance, it seems, he tried to make his way back to the cover of the armoured car. As the battle continued, the Republicans were reinforced when a party of Volunteers, who were making their way to the proposed brigade meeting, suddenly arrived on the scene.

The fight continued for at least a half an hour and as it was ending, Collins, for some unknown reason, stepped out onto the road in full view of the attackers. A shot rang out and he fell, mortally wounded. Seán O'Connell, a friend and colleague of Collins, quickly ran to his fallen leader with Emmet Dalton. He later said of that moment, 'With a dreadful fear clutching our hearts we found our beloved Chief and friend lying motionless firmly gripping his rifle.'[18] Collins died a short time later.

Realising the precarious position they were in, Dalton knew they needed to get away quickly. The firing had by then died down and Dalton, together with Seán O'Connell and the motor-cycle driver Smith, took Collins' body to the armoured car, and later transferred it to the touring car. Although the firing had almost stopped, the Republicans had not yet retreated and, unknown to Dalton, they had a clear view of what was happening. According to Bill Powell, who was with Hales, 'We knew somebody was either dead or badly injured.'[19]

Once Collins' convoy moved off, the Republicans dispersed.[20] They were tired and hungry and they still had to attend the council meeting. Liam Deasy, with a few men, went to Bill Murray's house, while Tom Hales, with some others, went to Jim Murray's house nearby.

Both groups discussed recent events, but as of yet, although they knew that someone had been shot, just who it was remained a mystery. Their mood was one of optimism. They had stood their ground and fought well. However, that all changed when word reached them just who it was that had been killed. At Jim Murray's house, Hales and Jim Kearney, amongst others, were just finishing their meal when they heard the news:

> ... a girl ran in saying, 'Do you know who's dead! Michael Collins!' One man grabbed his cap from his knee, and triumphantly threw it up. Again, a first reaction – one of the enemy. Tom Hales joined his hands, lowered his eyes and said

nothing. Then he blessed himself and remained with head bowed for some time. The other men around the table sensed the tension in the room.[21]

The men reassembled in Bill Murray's house, where the brigade council meeting was to be held. There, the feeling was not one of joy or optimism, but of sadness and loss, not just because a man who had once been a close friend to many of them was now dead, but also because they wondered what his death would mean. If there had been any hope of ending the Civil War on honourable terms, that hope was now gone with the death of Collins.

The meeting began at 9.30 p.m. Among those present were Liam Deasy, Tom Crofts, Tom Hales and Tadhg O'Sullivan.[22] It did not last long and the men went their separate ways. Tom Hales left the meeting with Deasy and Tadhg O'Sullivan. Deasy recalled:

... many of us left Murray's with heavy hearts. To those of us who had known Michael Collins personally, and there were many, his death was tragic; to Tom Hales, Tadhg O'Sullivan and myself who had known him intimately, our sorrow was deep and lasting. We parted without discussion of any kind.[23]

12

SUSPICION, ARREST
AND ASSASSINATION

Although news of Collins' death spread quickly through Republican circles, the same cannot be said of the National Army's lines of communication. It was not until 24 August, two days after the ambush, that Seán Hales received word of what had happened. John L. O'Sullivan recalled:

> Though we were in the area itself, we never even heard about Collins' death for two days. We left Bandon for Dunmanway the morning after we met him and we were in Dunmanway for two days before we heard this terrible news. I'll never forget – the one thing I'll never forget in my life – was the feeling everybody had when they heard of his death. Everybody was stunned, everybody was speechless, everybody was shocked.[1]

The news of his commander-in-chief's death would, without doubt, have had a great impact on Seán Hales. But, more tragically, he knew that it was highly unlikely that his younger brother Tom was not involved in the ambush. It did, after all, take place right in the heart of Tom's area of command.

O'Sullivan recalled Seán's reaction to the news of Collins' death. He stated:

> Together they had been interned in Frongoch for a number of months after the 1916 Rising and were always extremely close. Another question which was left unanswered for Sean was, where was his brother Tom that evening?[2]

Meanwhile, on the morning of 23 August, Tom Hales, who returned to Jim Murray's house, quite close to where the ambush had taken place, awoke to a most troubling situation. In the middle of the night, two of his companions, Jim Kearney and Timmy Sullivan, with a local man, had revisited the ambush site. While there, they found an officer's cap which was covered in blood and had a large bullet hole at the rear. The men did not know what to do and so took the cap to Hales, who, upon looking at it, noticed that not only was there blood on it but also human tissue. The only option Hales could think of was to bury it. At six o'clock that morning, Hales, Kearney and Sullivan, having found a suitable location in a field close to Murray's, prepared to bury the cap:

As the men now stood close to the oak tree, Hales, with the

aid of a penknife, carefully levered off the front badge and diamond. 'A souvenir of a friend,' he said sadly, and put it in his back pocket. He handed the cap to Kearney, who had dug a hole approximately a foot and a half deep. Kearney paused … 'The penknife!' he said, stretching out his hand to Hales … he severed the front strap from the officer's cap and put it in his pocket, but didn't speak.

Having completed the burial, Hales blessed himself; his two companions did likewise. Hales hesitated with bowed head. He had memories of his former friendship with Collins … As the men stood beside the buried cap, Tom Hales recalled his last conversation with Collins when Collins said, 'Sure we're all Republicans.'

Hales responded, 'Whatever you do, settle this thing.'

'I can't. There's no alternative,' said Collins.

'I'd find an alternative,' said Hales.

'What's the alternative?' Collins asked.

'Death!' said Hales. 'I'd die first.'[3]

A few days later, Jim Murray, whose house Tom Hales was staying in on the night of the ambush, dug up the cap, as the family kept pigs and cattle in the field and he feared they would dig it out. After he found the cap he took it home, washed it and put it safely away.

The Republicans looked set to have another success when, on 23 August, they kidnapped Collins' brother Seán, who was making his way to Cork city to accompany his brother's remains back to Dublin. What is most striking about this event is the fact that he was taken on the same road where his brother was killed. In an interview with *The Freeman's Journal*, he recounted the events: 'When we arrived at Bandon we were told that we must take the road to Macroom, as the main road was impassable, owing to the Irregular operations. About a mile outside the town we were fired upon.'[4] The car halted and a party of Republicans quickly surrounded them. Seán Collins continued:

We were asked to leave the car by one of these men, who in a jubilant manner, spoke of their having plugged 'Mickeen', meaning my brother.

Then one of the Irregulars intervened and put a stop to the controversy. We were carefully searched, but, of course, we were unarmed. We were then taken to a public-house, and one of the Irregulars offered us refreshments. We were detained until midnight ...

Shortly after midnight we were removed under a strong guard to a farmhouse, about a mile away, and the farmer made us as comfortable as possible ...

This morning, [Thursday 24 August] about 8 o'clock, breakfast was served, but I refused to take it. Tom Hales, the leader of the Irregulars, visited us during the night. We were released this morning.

All the Irregulars were highly delighted at having 'done in,' as they said, Mick Collins. They stated several times during the night that they would be very pleased to get 'Buckshot' Hales, meaning the elder brother of Tom ...[5]

This incident, and the threat made by the Republicans, must have been relayed to Seán Hales, who that evening, Thursday 24 August, accompanied Seán Collins, with General Tom Ennis, on a boat bringing Collins' remains back to Dublin. It seems most unlikely that the threats against Seán were made in the presence of Tom, but they were made nonetheless.

Seán Hales was present at the funeral of Michael Collins in Dublin on 28 August 1922. Throughout this time, while obviously dealing with his grief at such a loss, he must have been in turmoil about the ambush and his brother's role in it. Once the funeral was over, Seán returned to Bandon and began to make enquiries as to what exactly happened. Despite the fact that Seán and Tom were on opposite sides, they did remain in contact with each other and Tom had sent him a statement outlining the events surrounding the ambush. It was dated 22 August 1922 and in it Tom wrote that, 'The Column had pulled out of position and only a few men of a rearguard party were there when the car came in sight. They knew they had killed an officer of very high rank with one of the last shots fired but they had no idea who that officer was.'[6]

Some time passed before Seán received more evidence. By

chance he was in Lee's Hotel, by then the National Army headquarters, when a man named Ned O'Sullivan arrived with Collins' cap. Although Jim Murray had retrieved the cap from its burial place, he did not wish to keep it and so made arrangements for it to be given to the proper authorities. Immediately Hales recognised the cap, then 'he bowed his head and remained silent.'[7] Seán took it into his possession and told O'Sullivan that he would bring it to the proper authorities on his next visit to Dublin. He handed it over to the relevant people and it was given to the National Museum in 1932.[8]

Seán Hales became increasingly suspicious about the series of events that surrounded Collins' death. It has been said that he did not believe the official account of what happened. Whether this was due to an unwillingness on his part to believe that his brother and former colleagues were indeed responsible for Collins' death is not certain. However, it is easy to understand his reservations when it was discovered that there would be no inquest or proper inquiry held into Collins' death.

Regardless of his motives, Hales began to ask questions. Quite surprisingly, his efforts to discover the truth were ignored. He requested permission from his superiors to interview those who had been present at the ambush, but permission was denied. Despite these obvious obstructions,

Seán was not to be deterred and on a visit to Dublin he contacted army headquarters and a number of his fellow TDs in the Dáil to demand a full enquiry because 'he did not accept Emmet Dalton's version ... He was met with a blank refusal everywhere.'[9]

While Seán continued in his efforts to have an inquiry held, his younger brothers Tom, William and Robert were busy carrying on the Republican campaign. However, their chances of evading capture were diminishing due to increased National Army activity. On Friday 22 September William was arrested. A small announcement in the newspaper stated:

> On Friday evening Mr William Hales, brother of Mr Sean Hales, T.D., Brigade Commandant of the Free State forces, and of Mr Tom Hales, Brigade Commandant of the Republican forces, was arrested by National troops as he was about to make a short journey by boat along the County Cork [sic]. Two or three others were taken into custody with him.[10]

Events now followed that would change the way in which the Civil War was fought by both sides. On 5 September the Dáil had met in Dublin, where W. T. Cosgrave had been elected president of the Provisional Government and a cabinet had been formed that included Richard Mulcahy, now chief of staff of the army and Minister for Defence, and Kevin O'Higgins, Minister for Home Affairs. On 27

September the government introduced the Special Powers Bill, which gave special powers to the government, including the establishment of military courts which had the power to impose the death penalty on any person who was found carrying weapons or even ammunition.[11] A vote was taken in the Dáil and the Bill was passed. In response to this, the Republicans issued a warning to the government that anyone who voted for the 'Murder Bill', as they referred to it, was seen by them to be a legitimate target for assassination. The time for civility had now passed.

On 13 November Robert Hales was arrested in Newcestown. According to the entry in the Civil War prisoner internment ledgers, he was 'an active Irregular. Arrested near Newcestown by Capt. Higgins … Was connected in a robbery case near Ballineen. He had in his possession when arrested several money orders all stolen.'[12] It was only a matter of time before Tom would also be captured.

Finally, on 22 November, Seán heard that Tom had indeed been arrested. Whether he felt relief or despair on hearing the news is not known. Certainly, Tom's arrest was a great coup for the National Army. But the fact that he was now in custody did not guarantee his safety. After all, there was a lot of ill-feeling amongst the National Army towards the Republicans after the death of Collins and some must have been tempted to exact revenge on one of the men who had taken part in the ambush. It can be taken as a certainty that Seán would have feared for his brother's safety. Brendan Kelly's father, Paddy, was a captain in the National Army stationed in Bandon at the time of Tom's arrest, and told him as much. According to Brendan:

> Seán Hales was very concerned for his brother's safety being aware that there were always trigger-happy fanatics in every garrison. He went in search of Captain Paddy Kelly who had just arrived to his room in the Devonshire Arms Hotel after a gruelling and miserable day leading a flying column to outlying districts around Bandon. Seán Hales, who had befriended Paddy in recent times, asked him to escort Tom, his brother, to Cork [Victoria] Barracks as Tom Ennis wanted him brought there immediately. Seeing Seán's anguish and fearing that a situation of 'shot while trying to escape' might occur, Paddy agreed to take Tom and, along with a troop from 'E' Company, brought him on the long journey to Cork Barracks. On arrival [at] Victoria Barracks, the officer in charge refused to accept the prisoner without clearance from Headquarters. Paddy at this stage was close to drawing his gun on the officer but held his temper and managed to get the necessary authorisation, handed over the prisoner, and headed back on the long journey to Bandon.[13]

Word of Tom's arrest filled the newspapers, which reported that:

Troops from Comt.-Gen. Ennis's headquarters, Bandon, proceeded on Wednesday night to search a number of houses in Upton district. Whilst so engaged, a pony and trap were observed approaching. On the appearance of the troops the occupants of the vehicle, three in number, took flight, making their way across the fields.

The troops refrained from opening fire; but at once effected an encircling movement across the county. Despite a most minute search the military failed to get in touch with the fugitives. Still continuing their search the troops were returning to the main road and in a field discovered, concealed under a fence, Mr Tom Hales, the West Cork leader.

Mr Hales was in the act of destroying documents in his possession when apprehended. He was taken to Bandon and thence to Cork. Considerable importance is attached to the arrest and to the documents which have been found in his possession.[14]

According to the entry in the internment ledgers, Tom was a:

Prominent Irregular leader arrested at Knockvilla, Upton on 22/11/1922. He had in his possession 1 broken field glass and a note book which was blank and looked as if some pages were freshly torn out. He with four others deserted a trap in which they were driven and ran into the fields before being arrested.[15]

With his three brothers now in custody, Seán could concentrate his efforts on having an inquiry held into Collins' death. Jim Woulfe, who had been in Collins' convoy at the time of the ambush, and was afterwards appointed Hales' driver, recalled:

> After Michael Collins was killed at Béalnabláth [*sic*] I was appointed as General Seán Hales' driver by Captain Davy Coats who at the time was in charge of armoured-cars in Cork. Hales was allotted a Lancia armoured-car for West Cork. During the time I was driving him his chief topic of conversation was Michael Collins. He told me that he would leave no stone unturned until he got an inquiry or inquest held on Michael's death … At this time he was about three times in Dublin but all to no avail. The 'big brass' in Dublin would not listen to him. He told me himself and I can assure you he was a very disappointed man.[16]

Hales was not willing to let the matter go easily and on 6 December he made what was to be his last journey to Dublin. There is some controversy surrounding Seán's last movements. According to Vincent MacDowell in *Michael Collins and the Brotherhood*, Seán had stayed regularly in Portobello (Cathal Brugha) Barracks, the National Army Headquarters, when visiting Dublin, but on this occasion his driver was arrested for some unknown reason and, 'he [Seán] was told that there was no room for him in the barracks and that he would have to stay in a hotel that night'.[17] This version of events is also stated in John M. Feehan's *The Shooting of Michael Collins*, in which Feehan writes that, 'on one of the last evenings there he [Seán Hales] was told that they had no accommodation available for him, so he had to move to a hotel'.[18] In his book *On the Arm of Time*, Mícheal Ó Cuinneagáin also states that this happened.[19]

Although it is not certain why (or even if) Hales was turned away from the barracks, what is certain is that Seán did stay at the Ormond Hotel in the city centre. On the same day, the Dáil had convened to formally establish the Irish Free State, exactly one year after the signing of the Treaty, and Deputy Pádraig Ó Máille was elected as leas-cheann comhairle (deputy chairman). Ó Máille was a close personal friend of Hales and it has been stated that with a person like Ó Máille in the position of deputy chairman of the Dáil, Hales may have finally been able to push for a proper investigation into Collins' death. According to Vincent MacDowell:

They discussed how Hales' suspicions could be raised and agreed that Dáil Éireann should establish an inquiry, regardless of the Army or the Government, and this was to be moved the next day …

O'Maille [*sic*] agreed to call General Hales to address the Dáil on behalf of the Cork Command the next day [7 December], and accept a motion for an investigation. No one in the army or in the Council of Defence, knew that General Hales and the deputy speaker had decided on this step …[20]

The next day, Thursday 7 December, Seán met Ó Máille at the Ormond Hotel for lunch. Ó Máille's cousin, Patrick J. O'Malley, owned the hotel. There, it can be assumed, they discussed matters to be raised in the Dáil later that day. At 2.30 p.m. Hales and Ó Máille, having finished their lunch, left the hotel and hailed a hackney cab to bring them to Leinster House. As the cab arrived, Ó Máille's cousin went outside the hotel with them, where they met Senator Cohalan, a friend of Ó Máille's. Upon seeing this, O'Malley said his goodbyes and went back inside the hotel. Cohalan, Ó Máille and Hales engaged in a short conversation. Apparently, as they began to board the cab, Ó Máille turned back to speak to Cohalan while Seán continued to get inside. The time was now 2.45 p.m.

Unknown to Hales and Ó Máille, they were being watched by members of the Dublin No. 1 Brigade, anti-Treaty IRA. Almost as soon as Seán got into the cab, a number of shots rang out and he took the full force of the attack. Ó Máille was also hit. Immediately, Ó Máille shouted to the driver, John Kennedy, to, 'Get away as quick as you can.' At speed, Kennedy drove to Jervis Street Hospital, which was just a short distance away.

Present near the hotel was a British soldier, Lance Corporal Frederick Haynes, who saw the events unfold. He was driving an armoured car in the vicinity and noticed two men carrying revolvers running away from the hotel. As there was a British lorry passing by at the time, he assumed that they had attacked it. Unable to turn his car around, Haynes got out of his vehicle and pursued the men on foot, firing at them as he ran. At the inquest he stated:

> I jumped out and drew my revolver and called upon them to Halt. They took no notice but kept on running. I fired one round over their heads at the same time as I fired the shortest of the two Civilians turned into a side street on the left of Arran St. The other went down another street to the left, a matter of 15 yards between the two streets. I went back to my car as further pursuit was useless ... I would know the shortest of the two Civilians again. I have seen him daily when in charge of my car in town.[21]

Kennedy arrived at Jervis Street Hospital within minutes, but it was too late. At the time of their arrival at the hospital, at exactly 2.50 p.m., just five minutes after the shooting, Seán Hales was dead, 'struck down at the hand of a fellow-countryman'.[22]

13

AFTERMATH

News of Seán Hales' death spread rapidly, not just throughout Ireland but across the world. His younger brother Donal
was informed by telegram. It simply read: 'John Shot Dublin
Thursday = Desmond.'[1] In a letter to his sister, Donal spoke
of his hearing the news:

> With grief I read of the shooting of John and O'Maille [*sic*] in
> the Italian Press this morning.
>
> The soul is filled with horror at what is taking place in
> Ireland.
>
> I got a telegram from Dublin from Desmond Fitzgerald [*sic*]
> confirming what was published in the papers here. I can only
> hope that father and mother and you all will bear up bravely
> under this terrible blow.[2]

The Dáil was in session when the news was received. A journalist who was present wrote:

Suddenly an officer entered and there were whispers on the Government benches. It was apparent that some bad news had been passed to the members.

Mr Cosgrave then rose and in a voice trembling with emotion, the President said: 'I have just been informed a few moments ago that Deputy Seán Hales has been shot dead and Deputy Patrick O'Maille [*sic*] wounded. I need not say that on my own behalf and on behalf of the House that this is an appalling tragedy and that to the relatives of Deputy Hales we tender our sincere sympathy ...'

General Mulcahy, pale and angry, immediately jumped to his feet and taunted those deputies and others who have lately been demanding that men under sentence of death should be allowed to see relatives and priests and transact their private business before facing the unknown. There was no Press present, he said, in indignant tones, they [Hales and Ó Máille] were not asked if they would like to see their relatives or whether they would like to see a clergyman. They were not asked whether they had any private business of their own they would like to transact.[3]

The Free State government's response to the shootings was swift and severe. On the same day that the inquest was held into Seán's death, 8 December, four Republican prisoners, representing each of the four provinces of Ireland, were executed in Mountjoy Gaol: Dick Barrett, Joe McKelvey, Liam Mellows and Rory O'Connor. The execution of these men was an act of reprisal and illegal, a claim heavily denied by the government. Not one of the men had anything to do with the killing of Hales. All four had been in custody since the fall of the Four Courts in June that year and therefore could not and did not have anything to do with the assassination of Hales. They were not given the opportunity to defend themselves at a trial, they were simply chosen for who they were, with each man representing a province: Rory O'Connor for Leinster, Dick Barrett for Munster, Liam Mellows for Connaught and Joe McKelvey for Ulster. Their executions sent a clear message to the Republicans that the Provisional Government would uphold the Treaty at all costs and would do whatever it took to see the war through to its rightful conclusion. They, and not the Republicans, would be victorious.

But what was tragic about the executions of these men is the fact that not only had they all been acquaintances of those who had now sealed their fate, but Rory O'Connor was also a very close, personal friend of Kevin O'Higgins, Minister for Home Affairs. O'Connor had been best man at O'Higgins' wedding the year before. Sadder still was the fact that Dick Barrett was one of Seán Hales' closest friends. Barrett, a fellow West Cork man, had served in the Volunteers with Seán during the War of Independence. He was appointed quartermaster of the Third West Cork Brigade after Pat Harte was arrested with Tom in July 1920. The two had fought side by side in many ambushes and now both were dead. And just like Seán, as was so dramatically stated by Richard Mulcahy, the four men were not given the privilege of seeing their relatives before their executions.

Just as the Free State's response to the Hales killing was swift, so too was the response to their actions. The newspapers over the following weeks were filled with reports of condemnation from within the Dáil and various other public bodies throughout the country. The government was accused of acting in revenge. For example, Thomas Johnson, TD and leader of the Labour Party, when questioning President Cosgrave in the Dáil, stated:

> The four executed had been in [the] charge of the Government. The Government were charged with the care of these men. They thought well to try them, and then because a man who was held in honour was assassinated the Government of the country, the Government of Saorstat Eireann, announced apparently with pride that they had taken out the four men and as a reprisal for the assassination they murdered these men who could not have engaged in any conspiracy, as they had been in [the] charge of the Government for five months.[4]

The government was quick to respond to these accusations. Richard Mulcahy, Minister for Defence, stated that:

... the action taken that morning was not taken because a man had been assassinated whom they held in honour, or because Seán Hales, their comrade, had been assassinated. It was brought about by the fact that there were forces working around them more vicious and more insidious than Britain ever employed against representative Government in Ireland.[5]

The House and Finance Committee of Cork Mental Hospital also condemned the executions:

The shooting of Seán Hales would be condemned by any thinking Irishman, and they would also condemn the attitude of the Government who shot four men as a reprisal for the murder of Seán Hales – men who were his best friends and comrades in the late war ... It was for the people to speak out, and for the public Boards to give expression to their opinions, both on the shooting of Seán Hales and the execution of the other four men, and to tell the Government that they must do the will of the Irish people. He [Mr. R. Day] condemned the shooting of Seán Hales, and he condemned the execution of the other four men; everyone of them regretted the tragic deaths of brave men who fought together, and who he was sure, if they were spared, would fight again together against a common enemy.[6]

The most severe condemnation against the government's actions came from a most unlikely source: Seán's own family. In a letter sent to the editor of *The Cork Examiner* that they requested be published, they stated:

Sir – That we view with horror and disgust the execution of the four Irishmen, Richard Barrett, Liam Mellows, Joseph McKelvey and Rory O'Connor, as a reprisal for the death of Seán Hales, our dearly beloved brother, and we think it a criminal folly to believe that such methods will end the strife in our land; and we are of opinion that reprisals on either side will only increase the bitterness and delay the reconciliation that all patriotic Irishmen long and pray for, and also that the sole testimony of a British officer is very insufficient proof of how he met his death.

Signed Robert Hales	Father
Margaret Hales	Mother
Liam Hales	Brother
Domhnal Hales	Brother, Italian Consul, Genoa, Italy
Margaret Hales	Sister
Elizabeth Hales	Sister[7]

Seán Hales' remains were taken from the Pro-Cathedral, Dublin, on the evening of Saturday 9 December. As the funeral cortège passed through the city's streets, thousands of people turned out to pay their last respects. Soldiers, in formation, accompanied the coffin as the cortège made its way to the North Wall, where the remains would be taken by boat, the *Lady Kerry*, back to Cork. After lying in state in St Mary's Cathedral, he was buried in the family plot in Innishannon, a small village outside Bandon, on Monday 11 December 1922.

There were many moving scenes on this last journey. One such episode happened as the boat was just leaving Dublin: 'The military party accompanying the remains with a few friends of the deceased knelt round the coffin and in the twilight ... the Rosary was recited. It was ... strikingly reminiscent of the sad scenes enacted on the occasion of the transfer of the body of General Michael Collins to Dublin.'[8] Similar scenes were witnessed in Cork.

Possibly the most tragic aspect of Seán's funeral was not the fact that a mother and father had to bury their eldest son, but that Tom was not released from prison to pay his last respects to his older brother. The only explanation that can be given for this refusal is that to release Tom posed too big a risk for the authorities. He was at the time being held in Hare Park Camp in the Curragh. Robert was released on probation on the condition that he would return to custody on 16 December, which he failed to do. Tom did, however, write to his mother about the death of Seán:

My Dearest mother – As it was not possible for me to attend poor Seán's funeral, though it would be my wish, I pray God may strengthen and comfort you all under this terrible cross. I can quite understand the terrible shock you all received on hearing of poor Seán's death, and, moreover, in so brutal a fashion. Again, may God comfort you all and the country he loved. I myself am going on well. Your loving son, Tom.[9]

Seán Hales' death was felt on both sides of the divide, amongst his colleagues and former friends. Recalling the events, Liam Deasy wrote:

> The tragic news of those two days fairly shattered me … For twenty-four hours I could not think of nothing but the shooting of Sean Hales and that at the hands of my comrades. This was something for which I felt a personal responsibility as a member of the Executive that had made the order in October. The reprisals completed the tragedy and brought home the desperation and savage hate caused by this Civil War. Sean Hales and Dick Barrett, two of my most intimate and personal friends were now dead and for what?[10]

The army, in its tribute to Seán, stated:

> His loss will be mourned by every soldier of the Army of Ireland, by every man and woman who loves our country. The most fitting tribute we can pay his memory is to follow the example of his life, to give the same fearless and devoted service to Ireland as he gave. The bitterness of our bereavement will not stir up any spirit of mere vindictiveness against misguided men who are doing their utmost to destroy their country.[11]

Although these were very powerful and honourable words, that is all they were: words. As the Civil War entered its final phase in 1923, morality was replaced by savagery.

Determined to end the war quickly, the government became more ruthless, which in turn garnered a brutal response from the anti-Treaty IRA. In January alone, twenty-six Republicans were executed under the Special Powers Bill. The Republicans responded by escalating their attacks, culminating in the killing of National Army troops in Knocknagoshel, County Kerry, on 6 March 1923. The anti-Treaty IRA had booby-trapped an arms dump, which the troops, under Paddy 'Pats' O'Connor, went to investigate. He and four other soldiers were killed in the explosion. In the following days a total of seventeen Republican prisoners from the three Kerry brigades were deliberately murdered by members of the National Army.[12]

As the war dragged on, Tom Hales, with thousands of his comrades, remained in Hare Park. Conditions in this and the other camps in the Curragh were appalling. Alfred McLoughlin, who was a prisoner in Hare Park at the same time as Tom, wrote of the conditions he endured there:

In spite of what Gen. Mulcahy says, I slept on bare boards in the Curragh military prison for five nights – April 24–28 … I got one blanket … I was handcuffed night and day (day behind, night in front) … The handcuffs were not off for meals; they were off one wrist for alleged dinner, excluding Thursday, April 26, when they were both off for dinner, but on that day I was hanging handcuffed by the wrists to a kit-rack about six inches from the floor for four-and-a-half hours ... I was threatened with a gun several times [that] I was to be shot.[13]

The Civil War finally ended in May 1923, but for those in Free State custody the prospect of release was not forthcoming. At least 16,000 Republican prisoners were being held in prisons and internment camps all over the country. With no sign of conditions improving in the camps, and with no idea of whether or not they would be released, prisoners in Mountjoy Gaol went on hunger strike on 10 October 1923 in protest at their treatment. Frank Aiken, who had succeeded Liam Lynch as chief of staff of the IRA after Lynch's death in April 1923, issued an order for those in the camps to support their comrades in Mountjoy. In Hare Park and Tintown camps, nearly 3,500 men joined the hunger strike. Tom Hales, who was O/C of the prisoners in Hare Park at the time, wrote to the governor of the camp on 19 October:

Sir,

The Republican prisoners in this camp will go on Hunger Strike at 8 p.m., on Saturday evening, for unconditional release, in sympathy with our comrades and political leaders in Mountjoy Jail, upon whom your authorities are endeavouring to fix the status of criminals.

Every man in making this decision is clear within himself that the part he took in the recent war was prompted by the highest motive of patriotism, and by the faith which convinced him that to maintain the sovereignty of Ireland was his first duty as a soldier and an Irishman.

We realise that could your authorities succeed in Mountjoy Jail an endeavour would be made to fix the same status upon us, and our present action has, therefore, been forced upon us in order to defend our position and honour that of our comrades.

The efforts made since our internment in this camp to degrade us from the status of prisoners of war, coupled with our prolonged detention, and this latest attack upon our comrades, notwithstanding the fact that the military campaign ended several months ago, proves to us that it is not an admission of military defeat that is required from us, but a renunciation of the principle for which we have fought and for which we shall be always willing to sacrifice ourselves.

It is now six months since the cessation of hostilities was ordered by our leaders. That order has been faithfully obeyed and is accepted by all who now make the decision to sacrifice their lives rather than accept for themselves or their comrades the status of criminals.

Signed TOM HALES, Prisoners' O/C.[14]

The hunger strike continued for some time; however, unlike during the War of Independence, when it was a powerful tool used against the British government, the Free State government was not so quick to concede defeat. There were deaths amongst the strikers and with morale amongst the internees dwindling, it was eventually called off. The government did proceed to release the internees but it was a slow, well-planned and drawn-out process. If there was a general amnesty, it would be seen as a victory for the Republicans. Finally, by December 1924, after over two years in custody, Tom Hales was set free. However, just as it had been at the time of the Truce, when his brothers returned home having been on the run, the home that Tom was returning to was still trying to come to terms with recent events.

During his incarceration, not only had he suffered the loss of his older brother Seán, but one month after Seán's death, on 6 January 1923, their sister Hannah died. And in a tragic turn of events his father, Robert, the man who was responsible for instilling in his children a love of and pride for their country, passed away in September 1924, just a few months before Tom's release.

During the years 1920 to 1924, the Hales family had suffered severe hardships. Tom's incarceration in 1920, the family home being destroyed by the crown forces in 1921, the trauma of the Civil War dividing the family, Seán's death and the imprisonment of not just Tom, but also Robert and William, had placed a terrible burden on the family. After their home was destroyed, they were faced with the task of rebuilding, for which they did receive some compensation. However, after Seán's death their situation deteriorated rapidly. Seán was their main provider; their father, whose health deteriorated very quickly after the attack on his home, had been in a nursing home since March 1923 and the family was in dire need of financial support.

Seán's mother made claims not only to President Cosgrave, but also to Richard Mulcahy and other politicians and officials in the Department of Defence. For eight months, between August 1923 and March 1924, letters were sent to the various government departments in which Mrs Hales' solicitor pleaded her case very strongly, but compensation was slow to materialise. As one response from the army to President Cosgrave stated:

> I am directed by the Minister for Defence [Richard Mulcahy] to say that if, as stated, £500 has already been advanced in respect of this case he fears that there will be very little or no margin coming to his dependents out of any Claim they have lodged under the Pensions Act – especially in view of the fact that Brig. Hales was not a married man.[15]

The family did manage to survive, and with Tom now released there was at least a chance that they could return to some kind of normality. However, although they had no other choice but to carry on, the effects of the years of conflict stayed with the surviving members of the Hales family for a lifetime.

CONCLUSION

There has been much speculation over the years as to who killed Seán Hales and why. Certainly, there is still some controversy surrounding his death. Some historians, including Vincent MacDowell and Mícheal Ó Cuinneagáin, believe Seán's death occurred because of his demands for a full investigation into the death of Collins. Was it in fact true that he, a brigadier general of the National Army, had been turned away from army headquarters the night before his death? And if this did in fact happen, then why? Unfortunately, it has not been possible to find definite proof of this, as the Free State government, before leaving office in 1932, deliberately destroyed many official records regarding policy, executions and reprisals during the Civil War.

There is, however, ample proof that Seán's killing was committed by the IRA, and that his death may have been accidental. Liam Deasy stated that his death was because of the IRA Executive's order to target anyone who had voted for the Special Powers Bill. Seán, although a TD, was not present on the day the Dáil voted on the bill and so had nothing to do with it being passed. This begs the question: was it in fact Pádraig Ó Máille who was the real target of the assassination and not Seán? Ó Máille had voted in favour of the bill and he was with Seán on the day of the shooting. According to *The Irish Times*, 'there was a strange resemblance between him [Hales] and Padraig Ó'Máille [*sic*]. Hales was fair, while O'Maille is dark, but both were huge men, with rugged faces and heavy slowly-moving limbs.'[1] And, as was stated, Ó Máille had made his way onto the hackney carriage but got off to speak to a colleague, whereupon Seán took his seat. Thus, when the firing started, Seán bore the full onslaught of the attack. A letter from the Dublin No. 1 Brigade to the adjutant general of the anti-Treaty IRA recounted the events:

Sean Hales, F.S. T.D. and officer of F.S. Army shot dead –
Unintentionally – while in company with P. O'Maille [*sic*]. It was intended only to wound Hales, but he was mistaken for O'Maille.
... it is fairly certain that what happened was:
that O'Maille was pointed out as our men were under cover in a lane way and during the few seconds while O'Maille turned back to speak to a friend he exchanged places with Hales and owing to their general appearance being somewhat similar the mistake was made ... You will realise however that it was not intended to shoot Hales at the time as O/C Dublin 1 reports. The intention was only to wound him ...[2]

Further information regarding Seán's death came to light in 1985 at a performance of Ulick O'Connor's play *Execution*, in Dublin, which tells the story of the executions that took place in Mountjoy in response to Seán's killing. O'Connor wrote in his diary that on the night of 11 November 1985 he was accosted by an old man who wished to discuss the events that O'Connor depicted. He recalled:

> The little man says he knows who shot Sean Hales, the TD whose death was the cause of the executions.
>
> 'How do you know?'
>
> 'I was the Intelligence Officer for the anti-Treaty forces during that time and I took the official report from the man who had just shot him. It was about an hour or two after it happened.'
>
> … I asked him to tell me who was the killer who had made the report to him. He said it was a young man called Owen Donnelly who came from Glasnevin.
>
> 'Who ordered him to do it?' I asked.
>
> 'No one gave him an order,' he said. 'At that time the general orders issued by Liam Lynch were for anybody to shoot TDs or Senators if they could.' He said Donnelly was a … fair-haired fellow who had been a very good scholar in O'Connell Schools. The little man said he had also been at O'Connell's with Donnelly. Donnelly was of a good background …
>
> He (Sean Caffrey was his name) was in the main room of the Intelligence Centre when Donnelly came in shortly after the killing, on the afternoon of December 7, 1922 …[3]

From these documents it can be assumed that Seán's assassination was indeed carried out by the IRA, and it is doubtful that he was the intended target. He had, after all, *not* voted for the Special Powers Bill so it is unlikely that he would have been a deliberate target for assassination by the anti-Treaty forces. The author of the letter to the adjutant general quoted above states that Seán was shot 'Unintentionally – while in company with P. O'Maille [*sic*].'

What is certain is that Seán's death had a terrible effect on his family. Madge, in a letter to Donal, wrote of their plight:

> I wish you would see poor Tom's letter on poor Seán's death, and on his life … Tom feels it terribly … Father is in hospital in Blackrock, poor dear man has suffered more than his share. Oh to see him waiting for poor Seán to come to see him, he was extremely fond of his father. Oh to think that never more will he come. How great is our trial, poor Seán was … like a loving father to us all, anyone of us need only ask him always for anything and he would take pleasure in giving it, his heart was large enough to love the whole world, how the poor and humble mourn his loss, his good works are living after him. Ah Ireland have cause to mourn the loss of such men.[4]

After the executions of the four men in Mountjoy Gaol on 8 December, Donal Hales stated:

My brother would be the last to tolerate the inhuman act and in life, affirmed the heart of the Republican movement to the men of … pure ideals, disinterested in purpose, without personal ambition and like himself struggling for the complete independence of their country.[5]

In the years following the end of the Civil War, the Hales family, like thousands of families across the country, tried to rebuild their lives after nearly a decade of conflict. Unfortunately for many, the events of the previous years had taken their toll, and as more information about these men and women is revealed it is no surprise to find that many suffered from some form of post-traumatic stress.

Tom Hales seems to have made the readjustment to normal life quite successfully, which is surprising considering all he had been through. In 1928 he married Anne Lehane from Kilmichael. They had been friends for many years and the couple had five children: three boys, Seán, Robert and Tom, and two girls, Eileen and Peggy. They lived at the family home in Knocknacurra, which had been rebuilt. Tom continued to be active in politics and was a member of Cork County Council from 1924 until 1942. A member of Fianna Fáil, he was elected to Dáil Éireann from 1933 until 1937, when he resigned as a member of the party in protest against what he viewed to be Éamon de Valera's coercive policy against his former comrades in the IRA, who were continuing in their efforts to achieve full independence. His concern for the welfare of farmers was something that never left him and he was involved with many farmers' associations, including the Mallow Area Board of the Beet Growers' Association.

Tom Hales died on 29 April 1966. He was seventy-four years old. Hundreds attended the funeral, including many of his comrades from the Third West Cork Brigade, who marched in the funeral procession to St Patrick's Cemetery, Bandon.

In their aim to win independence, Seán, Tom and indeed the whole Hales family made great sacrifices, just like the many thousands of families in Ireland at that time. But the price of achieving that freedom was indeed a high one to pay. They had shared in the excitement of battle, the hardship of imprisonment and torture and the destruction of their family home. They endured the bitter divide of the Civil War, and unfortunately were reluctant participants in two of the most tragic events of that conflict, the after-effects of which are still felt in Ireland today. Both sincerely desired only peace, as their sister Madge recalled:

Did you hear of the meeting poor Sean [*sic*] and Tom had on peace. Oh what bright hopes they had after that meeting … they spent a whole night together. Tom says to his dying day he will thank God for that their last meeting, poor dead Seán R.I.P. was foully murdered soon after ... Oh if he was spared what they would have done together towards peace.[6]

The brothers never lost their respect for each other:

During the civil strife, somebody thinking that they would please Tom came to him and ran down Seán (who was then still alive) and praised himself. Tom told them clear ... that himself could never persevere to be like Seán, he also told him that in Ireland there was not another who had Seán's personality and his noble record.[7]

But was this desire to achieve freedom worth the amount of suffering that they endured? As one comrade wrote, remembering the sacrifices made by the Hales family, 'they placed their all on the altar of their country'.[8] That, it seems, was the price they were willing to pay.

MAP OF THE WEST CORK BRIGADE AREA

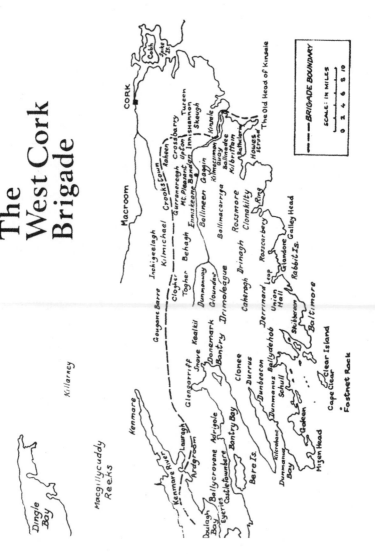

The West Cork Brigade

Reproduced from Meda Ryan, *Tom Barry: IRA Freedom Fighter* (Mercier Press, Cork 2003)

Appendix 2

Oath of Allegiance to Dáil Éireann 1919

'I, A.B., do solemnly swear (or affirm) that I do not and shall not yield a voluntary support to any pretended Government, authority or power within Ireland hostile and inimical thereto, and I do further swear (or affirm) that to the best of my knowledge and ability I will support and defend the Irish Republic and the Government of the Irish Republic, which is Dáil Éireann, against all enemies, foreign and domestic, and I will bear true faith and allegiance to the same, and that I take this obligation freely without any mental reservation or purpose of evasion, so help me, God.'

Source: http://oireachtasdebates.oireachtas.ie/debates authoring/debatesweb pack.nsf/takes/dail191908200013?opendocument

APPENDIX 3

PRESENTATION TO THE AMERICAN COMMISSION ON CONDITIONS IN IRELAND

The following testimony forms part of the 'Evidence on Conditions in Ireland, Comprising the Complete Testimony, Affidavits, and Exhibits Presented before the American Commission on Conditions in Ireland', published in May 1921.[1] The commission was established to find out the truth about what was happening in Ireland. It was an impartial committee consisting of 150 individuals from a broad section of society, five of whom set up a public enquiry in Washington DC with a view to discovering what the situation was in Ireland. Members of the committee visited Ireland in late 1920 to see for themselves the realities of what was being reported and, in many cases, as with Tom Hales, affidavits were collected reporting on acts carried out against individuals in British custody. The commission did not have the official backing of the American government. In the case of Tom Hales, Lord Mayor of Cork Francis Doyle read out his statement. Doyle had succeeded Terence MacSwiney as lord mayor on his death in October 1920, having been on hunger strike in Brixton Prison, England, for seventy-five days.

BARBAROUS TORTURE OF IRISH PRISONERS

There have been a number of cases where ill-treatment after arrest has been alleged. But as that has been a more or less recent development, and as the men in whose cases it has been alleged are still nearly all in jail, it has not been possible to get the particulars in a number of cases. Fortunately, in one case, and I think it is a most glaring as well as a most cruel case, we have got the deposition, although the man in this particular case is still in prison.

The man concerned is Thomas Hales, one of the Hales family from Knocknacurra, near Bandon, County Cork. It is a family who are famous as athletes. His brother represents the Irish Republic as consular agent there [Italy]. I had the pleasure of meeting him last July when I was there. I will read the deposition of Thomas Hales:

Affidavit of Thomas Hales

'On the 27th July, 1920, at about 5 p.m., I was standing outside a farmhouse at Laragh, about two and three-quarter miles from Bandon, — Mr Hurley is the proprietor of the house. Some police and soldiers came and surrounded the house and took me and Harte. I was brought inside the house, and there saw Captain Kelly with other military officers.'

The Witness: Captain Kelly, I might explain, is one of

193

the intelligence officers attached to the British Military Headquarters at Cork.

'I had no coat on at the time. They then took me into an outhouse, and took all my other clothes off me and searched them for documents. They found some documents on me and on searching my coat, which was hanging up, they spilt out of it some cartridges. I had no cartridges in my possession, and I'm of the opinion that these were placed there by the military. Captain Kelly and Lieutenant Keogh took all my clothes off me. Lieutenant Keogh said, "You have documents with regard to the boycott of the R.I.C." When I was undressed they strapped my hands behind my back with leather straps, and put them around my neck and mouth. Harte was also strapped in a similar position. I was not in a position to defend myself, and Lieutenant Keogh hit me several times in the face and on the body. Kelly said, "You have some documents from the Adjutant General per Michael Collins." He apparently assumed that M. C. stood for Michael Collins. They dressed me again, tied my hands behind my back with leather straps, and also dressed Harte. Kelly said, "You will be shot." They put straps around my legs as well as round Harte's legs. They made me stand up, and made Harte stand behind me. They discovered a slab of gun-cotton in the farm. I do not know whether it was brought in by the military or not. They placed the gun-cotton on Harte's back, strapped it there, and Kelly said, "Be prepared for a shock." They looked round for a detonator, but could not find one. They then took the gun-cotton off Harte's back, and while my hands were strapped behind my back, and Harte's hands were also strapped behind his back, Lieutenant Keogh hit me and Harte in the face several times. He hit me very hard, and he had in his hand, I believe, the butt end of a revolver.

'They then tied my right leg to Harte's left leg, and marched us off to a lorry about 200 yards away, I was prodded by a bayonet, and I was hit in the nose by the butt end of a gun. I was very weak, and it was difficult to walk in a three-legged fashion.

'There were two girls in the farm who witnessed some of what took place, namely, Miss Hurley and Miss Lordan. I am not certain if they were in the outhouse when I was stripped, but if they were not in the outhouse they were certainly outside. There were other people present who could also verify what took place. One of the boys of the farm was arrested at the same time, but the military let him go.

'On reaching the lorry, they were not able to throw us both in together, so they separated Harte from me, and they threw us into the lorry. I was nearly blind, as blood was running down my face from the injuries I had received. We were taken to Bandon into the Military Barracks yard, and were lined up to be shot. The soldiers were howling for our death, and were anxious to shoot us. We had our backs to the wall, and Harte was on my left-hand side. Keogh said. "Do you want to be blindfolded?" We said, "No." I asked to see a chaplain. Keogh said, "Damn it, why do you want to see a chaplain?" I said, "All right, go ahead."

'We were still tied with our hands behind our backs, and the soldiers hit us with their fists. My sight was getting very dim, owing to the blood that I was losing, and I felt very weak.

'Kelly paced out twelve to fifteen paces from us, and then put five or six men with rifles at the end of the fifteen paces. Harte was then very weak and could hardly see. He stuck a flag into Harte's hand, and made him hold his hand up. I recognized that the flag Harte was holding up was the Union Jack, but Harte himself was too far gone to recognize it. A man came with a camera and took a snapshot. Kelly then said, "We must get some information first before we shoot them." We were then taken across the Barracks yard into a room in the Barracks. The soldiers were furious at not being allowed to shoot us, and they punched us and pummelled us the whole way across the yard.

'They locked us into a room. It was getting dark by this time. About midnight I was led out by the guard, and taken to an upper room. There were, I believe, six officers in this room, including Captain Kelly of the enemy Military Intelligence

Department, stationed at Cork City; Lieutenant Keogh of the Hants Regiment; Lieutenant Richardson, in charge of wireless at Bandon; Lieutenant Green, believed to be of the Hants Regiment. They were sitting down as if they were going to try me. There were no soldiers, only officers in the room.

'Kelly opened the proceedings by saying, "We are going to try you." My hands were still tied behind my back, and the strap was fastened round my neck and face. Kelly took up a book which he said was a Bible, and opened it and placed it in my hands behind my back. He told me to repeat the oath which he was going to say. I said, "For what purpose?" He said, "We want your name, and for you to answer other questions on oath. If you do not, you will be handed over to the R.I.C., and they will quickly identify you and deal with you." I, of course, was well known to Captain Kelly. He had seen me many times before, and of course knew my correct name. I had previously given a false name when I was arrested — that was before I knew Kelly was present.

'I said, "I have no objection to giving my name." They let my trousers and pants round my feet, my hands still being behind my back. "Now," said Kelly, "repeat the following words after me." He then started saying some form of oath and included in it the name of the Blessed Virgin. I did not repeat the name of the Blessed Virgin, and two of the officers took their canes and beat me on my bare legs for about five minutes. I was powerless to do anything. Kelly then asked my name. I said, "Tom Hales." He said, "You are Commander of a Brigade." I said I was one time. He asked me who was the man next in command to me. I said I refused to tell him. I said, "You are foreigners to me, but I appeal to you, if you are gentlemen, to go ahead and get on with the shooting part of it. I am quite ready."

'Kelly then told one of the officers to go out and get the pliers. He then said, "You are an anarchist and a murderer. You have organized all the murder and attacks on barracks in this part of the country." He said, "Where were you on Sunday? Were you at mass, and at what mass?" I said, "I was at mass at Rossmore." He then asked me was I not responsible for raising the training camp at Glandore last year. I refused to answer. The two officers then gave me about forty cuts each on my bare legs. Kelly then said, "Will you refuse to tell me was Professor Gerald Sullivan Commander of the camp?" I told him I did not know such a man. He said, "You are a damned liar." The two officers then gave me vicious blows on the leg, and the blood was flowing down my legs from several wounds in them. (Dr Shannon, civilian doctor of Cork Prison, saw the scars that were on my legs.) The scars were visible for three weeks after this night's event.

'Kelly said, "There was one of your dispatches intercepted connected with the camp and signed by you. Be sure we know more about you than you think." Then he said, "Where did you sleep last Sunday night?" I said, "I was at home." "That is a damned lie," said Kelly. I said, "I generally sleep at home. I hardly ever sleep in anybody else's house. The hay shed is good enough for me." Kelly said, "You organized and were in the attack on Farnivane Police Barracks." I said, "You may have been told that." He asked me what rank did John Buckley of Bandon hold in the Irish Republican Volunteers. I said, "He is a builder, and a good Sinn Feiner at that." I was again viciously whipped for the statement. He said, "What position does your brother John hold and where is he staying?" I said, "I refuse to give you any information about him." He then turned to the officer whom he had sent for the pliers, and he started bending and twisting and pinching my fingers at the back. He gripped them at the back, placing one portion of the pinchers against one side of my nail and the other portion of the pinchers against the other. He brought the blood to the tops of several of my fingers, and for some time afterwards my fingers were black on the tops, owing to congealed blood there. I was feeling extremely weak, almost fainting, and the blood was dropping down my legs. I was asked several questions about other individuals and about military matters, but I refused to give any information.

'Kelly also put the pinchers on my thighs, but my senses were becoming quite numb. After that, and finding I would answer no questions, he told me I would be shot at dawn. He said, "You are a Commander of a Brigade and know all about these murders. If you do not know, you should know, or you can have no control over your men." I said, "If that is so that I have no control over my men, there are other people besides me that have no control over their men."

'Keogh then untied my hands and told me to pull up my trousers. I did so, and my trousers were sopping wet with blood. Kelly said, "The Court is closed for the finding." He said, "Stand up," as my knees were somewhat bending, "and we will see what a Tommy can do to you." Keogh then landed me a terrific punch in the face. I said I would not defend myself; I would not give them an excuse to say I had hit them. Keogh hit me several times in various parts of the body, but especially in the face, and he broke the four teeth in my upper jaw. He then knocked me down on the ground. I was absolutely exhausted and nearly fainted, and my senses were beginning to go. He hit me on several occasions while I was on the ground. After a few minutes one of the officers said, "That's enough." I was then dragged up and led out of the room. My hands had not been retied since they had been undone in order to lift up my trousers. When I got outside my hands were tied up again and the straps fastened round my neck and face. Five or six soldiers hit me while I was going to the room where Harte was.

'After I had been placed in this room, bleeding and exhausted, Harte was taken upstairs. He was treated in a very similar fashion, and it has, unfortunately, had a detrimental effect upon his brain, and he is now practically mentally incapacitated.

'In the morning, at daybreak, the 28th July, the sergeant came in and loosened the straps that tied my arms. About half an hour afterwards Captain Kelly came in with a squad of men and took me out of the room. He noticed the straps were not tight. He said, "Who in the hell loosened your straps?" He had them immediately tightened. I went into another room and had to kneel down. Harte was also brought in and told to kneel down; and we were left kneeling for about five minutes. We were then told to get up, and were taken into the barrack yard. They put me up against a wall. I said, "Will you let me see a chaplain?" "No," said Kelly, "I will not." I said to Kelly, "Your life will only be a short one, the same as mine."

'He immediately drew out an automatic pistol and placed it against my temple and said, "One question, and on the answer of this question depends your life. Give me the names of the six battalions." I said, "Even if I knew the names of the six battalions, I would not tell you." Kelly said, "I will give you another chance, and if you don't tell me the battalion names, I will shoot you dead." I said, "Go on. I won't tell you the names."

'He then took down the revolver and walked over to where some of the officers were, and said something to them. I then heard him say, "We will take him off, and we will give him some more torture." They threw me into a motor lorry. Harte was also thrown into the same motor lorry, and we were brought to the Military Hospital in Cork. I was attended to by the doctor in the hospital, and my treatment and Harte's treatment in the hospital was satisfactory. We were given newspapers and were not in any way molested or struck, and our injuries were attended to.

'We were placed, though, in a ward where there were twelve wounded policemen, and they were all day and all night long talking at us and crying for our blood. This had a very detrimental effect upon Harte, who in consequence is now in a very weak mental state.

'On Tuesday, the 19th August, we were told by the military officer that we would be tried by court-martial sharp at 10 o'clock. On August 20th, at [a] quarter to ten, we were taken to the place where the court-martial was to take place. After waiting for half an hour, the sergeant was told to take us back, as the court-martial was postponed. At twelve o'clock we were taken again to the same place, and again, after waiting half an hour, the court-martial was postponed and we were taken back. At 2.30 we were taken again to the court-martial, and the court-martial took place. I refused to recognize the court, and I refused to cross-examine, but I stated that I had no munition [*sic*] on me. The president asked me did I want to cross-examine Captain Kelly. I said, "No." We were sentenced to two years' hard labor.'

The Witness: Well, that, gentlemen, is one of the most glaring cases I know of.

CRUELTY DRIVES PRISONER INSANE

Q. *Senator Norris:* That man is still in prison serving his time?
A. Yes, sir; that man is still in prison serving his two years. And in the case of the man Harte, we have had reports definitely, — we have heard rumors, but some time before I left we learned that the poor man had lost his mental balance and was insane. We made efforts before I left Cork to get him transferred to the Cork lunatic asylum, but up to the time I left, nothing came of it.

Q. *Mr Doyle:* Was this affidavit admitted to the Labor Commission which was in Ireland?
A. Not that I know of. Not in Cork. It may have been in Dublin.

Q. Were some affidavits submitted?
A. Some of them were.

Q. *Commissioner Thomas:* That Captain Kelly is still in the Information Office?

A. In Cork, he is.

Q. Is Captain Kelly an Irishman?
A. That I do not know. I know nothing whatever of him. I scarcely think he would be, and I surely hope not.

Q. *Commissioner Maurer:* This party you were telling about, in what prison is he?
A. In Dartmoor, I think.

Q. That prison is in England?
A. Yes, sir.

Q. *Commissioner Wood:* Do you know these persons, Mr Lord Mayor?
A. Not all of them.

Q. Were these depositions made before you in your position as chief magistrate of the city of Cork?
A. Yes, sir, most of them were.

Q. *Senator Norris:* This one you just read was?
A. Well, that was an irregular one. Most of these poor men are still in prison. That is the case of this particular man whose affidavit I have just read, Mr Tom Hales. He is still in

prison; and that had to be given through channels other than the ordinary deposition. But it is perfectly reliable.

Q. *Chairman Wood:* Do you know that man yourself?
A. Yes, I know him personally.

Q. *Senator Norris:* He is a reputable man in every way?
A. Oh, yes, absolutely.

Q. How old a man is he?
A. Thirty-five or thirty-seven. His father is a farmer in a large way near Bandon. He has three or four brothers. They have a threshing machine which they operate all around there.

Q. How long have you known him?
A. Five or six years.

Q. He bears a good reputation, does he?
A. Yes, as good as any man in the country. ...

ABUSE OF PRISONERS A VIOLATION OF RULES OF WAR

Q. *Commissioner Thomas:* Before you leave the Hales case, may I ask a question or two?
A. Certainly.

Q. Mr Hales was sentenced for two years?
A. Yes.

Q. Do you happen to know on what ground he was sentenced?
A. No, for the moment I do not know definitely what the charge was. I think it was for having seditious documents in his possession. The two charges usually are either for having seditious documents or for having arms and ammunition in your possession.

Q. Do I understand that Mr Hales admitted quite openly his membership in, and the fact that he had held a commission in the Republican Army?
A. Yes.

Q. If Mr Hales had been treated as an ordinary prisoner of war, would he have objected?
A. No, he would have been quite satisfied.

Q. You see, the fact that I would like to bring out, and which I think you would like to impress upon us, is the treatment of this prisoner [is] not in accordance with the rules of warfare.
A. No, of course, it was his treatment subsequent to arrest, when he was a prisoner.

Q. But the fact was not disputed that he was an officer in the Republican Army?

A. No, no.

Q. And as an officer in that army, he would, of course, have taken part in the operations of that army?

A. Yes, of course, and would have been willing to take the consequences; and the consequences, of course, should have been in accordance with some legitimate method of treatment, and not in the barbarous manner in which he was treated in this case.

APPENDIX 4

LETTER FROM M. O'SHANAHAN REGARDING HIS TREATMENT OF TOM HALES AFTER HIS TORTURE

34 South Mall

Cork

March 19th 1924

I remember Mr T. Hales being brought to Central Military Hospital back when I was Surgical Specialist there. He had some front teeth broken and several loosened. His face was badly bruised and swollen. His body and legs were black and blue nearly all over and marks of sticks in several places. There was also dried blood on his shirt and trousers. He seemed to be suffering from shock also.

M. O'Shanahan M.D.

Source: Florence O'Donoghue Papers, MS 31323, National Library of Ireland.

APPENDIX 5

BRITISH RESPONSE TO HALES' STATEMENT

Thomas Hales, fiction and fact

On October 15th the 'Irish Bulletin', a typewritten circular issued by Sinn Fein propaganda department to their branches in the country and also to all available British and foreign newspaper correspondents, gave a malicious and untrue account of the pretended torture of Thomas Hales, an active member of the franctireur murder gangs described as the 'Irish Republican Army', by members of His Majesty's forces in Ireland.[1] Publicity has been given both in Gt Britain and abroad to this narrative said to have been written by Hales and declared to be the 'simple statement of a man whose integrity and truthfulness down to the smallest detail are above question'. It is significant that this statement about an event said to have taken place on July 27th is delayed until one of the officers (Lieut. Richardson R.A.F.) against whom the charges are brought has been assassinated and is no longer able to defend himself against the accusations. The officer in question was Lieutenant Richardson, R.A.F.

Hales is declared in the statement to have been bound and

gagged with straps, to have been hit repeatedly in the face by Officers and to have had a sort of thumb-screw torture applied by means of pliers.

A full official enquiry has been made into the charges contained in the published narrative. The facts are as follows: Patrick Harte and Thomas Hales were arrested at the farmhouse of Frank Hurley at Laragh near Bandon on the afternoon of July 27th 1920.

Thomas Hales was Commandant of the Third West Cork Brigade, Irish Republican Army, and Patrick Harte was Quartermaster of the same Brigade, and believed to be concerned in the assassination of Sergt. Mulhern [sic], RIC in the Roman Catholic Chapel at Bandon on July 26th.

The former was concerned, as he admitted, as leader in the attack on Mount Pleasant Barracks and other murderous outrages in the West Riding of County Cork. On arriving at the farmhouse the officer in charge of the military detachment which make [sic] the arrests found a lady's bicycle with a small handbag. In the handbag was a dispatch of the Irish Republican Army addressed to the 'O/C No. 1 Battalion'.

Inside the house were two women, one of them being identified now by the *Irish Bulletin* as Miss Lordan.[2] At the time she gave a false name and declared that the bicycle was not her property, though she subsequently made an attempt to ride away on it. Thomas Hales and Patrick Harte were found behind the farmhouse. On being arrested and asked their names they both gave false names and addresses. They were placed under escort while the officer went in to search the house. During his absence Hales after an attempt to escape was insulting to the sentry guarding him and called him 'an English Bastard'. The sentry hit him in the mouth. The sentry further reported having seen Hales and Harte attempting to hide papers in a hedge. The hedge was searched and a number of documents with the Irish Volunteers etc. were found.

Hales was now searched and in order to do so he was taken to an outhouse and made to take off some of his clothing. Ammunition and documents were found on his person. To ensure his safe custody his hands were tied behind him but his feet were not tied nor was any unnecessary force employed. Harte's hands were tied with a piece of strap there being no handcuff available.

In the meantime the woman named Miss Lordan had taken her departure and as a considerable number of persons were gathering and the military force was small the prisoners were put into a lorry with the ammunition, documents, etc., discovered, and taken to Bandon. The prisoners were neither tied together nor were they in any way illtreated [*sic*] despite the insolence they displayed.

On arrival at Bandon Military barracks the prisoners' hands were untied and they were taken into barracks. They were however recognised by some of the soldiers in barracks who were at the time infuriated by the cowardly murders of Sergeant Mulhern RIC and Corporal Maddock of the First Essex Regt. They received a few severe blows in the face and body but the men were immediately ordered to desist and did so. For their own safety the prisoners were placed in a barrack room under a special guard. Subsequently the men were formally interrogated and charged after being duly cautioned. Hales was asked to explain a document found on him containing a number of names and addresses of Commandants of Battalions and officers of companies in the 3rd West Cork Brigade of which he was commandant. He also admitted that he led the attack on Mount Pleasant Police Barracks. Harte was similarly charged, cautioned and questioned. At first he refused to answer but he subsequently admitted that he was Quartermaster of the 3rd West Cork Brigade and took his orders from Hales.[3] He also said 'I would shoot any policeman or anyone else if I was ordered to do it by the Irish Republic'.

Neither then nor subsequently were the men ill-treated in any way. The only blows they received were those already mentioned above. The story of torture applied to extract evidence is a pure fabrication.

Hales and Harte were conveyed to Cork and placed in the Main GuardRoom [sic] at Victoria Barracks. They were visited there by an officer on the morning of July 28th and asked if they had any complaints to make. They said they had not. Hales said that his mouth was sore and Harte's face appeared slightly swollen so they were removed to the Military Hospital Detention Ward.

A Hunger Strike started in the Civil Gaol a few days later and in order to prevent their association with the Hunger Strikers and to prevent them doing the same they were detained in the Hospital until tried by District Court Martial. At the trial they were again asked if they wished to crossexamine [*sic*] any of the witnesses or to make any statement. Hales asked one of the searchparty [*sic*] if he (Hales) was wearing his coat at the time ammunition was found on him but otherwise they refused to crossexamine any witnesses.

The evidence as to the identity of his associates given by the convict Hales has subsequently been acted upon by the authorities and there is no doubt that this fact has come to the knowledge of his associates who would have every reason to endeavour to discredit the information received, as also would Hales wish to cover up any betrayal of his comrades. The charges made against the officer carrying out the arrest follow upon a long series of attempts to remove him by assassination, intimidation and so forth. The issue of the present fabrication has probably been influenced by the hope that the officer in question might be _____ under the pressure of misinformed public opinion.

Source: National Archives Ireland, CO 904/168.

APPENDIX 6

FREE STATE CONSTITUTION

Article 17
Oath of Allegiance

The oath to be taken by members of the Oireachtas shall be in the following form:–

I .... do solemnly swear true faith and allegiance to the Constitution of the Irish Free State as by law established, and that I will be faithful to H.M. King George V, his heirs and successors by law, in virtue of the common citizenship of Ireland with Great Britain and her adherence to and membership of the group of nations forming the British Commonwealth of Nations.

Such oath shall be taken and subscribed by every member of the Oireachtas before taking his seat therein before the representative of the Crown or some person authorised by him.

APPENDIX 7

SPECIAL POWERS (EMERGENCY)
BILL, 26 SEPTEMBER 1922

Whereas the Government has entrusted to the Army the duty of securing the public safety and restoring order throughout the country, and has placed on the Army the responsibility for the establishment of the authority of the Government in all parts of the country in which that authority is challenged by force:

And Whereas the Army authorities have represented to the Government that in order to discharge effectively the duty and responsibility so placed on them it is essential that the Army authorities should have power to establish Military Courts or Committees, with full powers of enquiring into charges and inflicting punishment on persons found guilty of acts calculated to interfere with or delay the effective establishment of the authority of the Government, and that the Army authorities should have power to detain in places whether within or without the area of the jurisdiction of the Government persons arrested by the Army authorities, and power to control the dealing in and possession of firearms:

And Whereas the Government, recognising the force of such

representation, has sanctioned the doing by the Army authorities of all or any of the following matters and things:–

(a) The setting up of Military Courts or Committees for the enquiring into charges against persons in respect of any of the offences hereinafter mentioned, provided however that every such Military Court or Committee shall include as a member thereof at least one person nominated by the Minister of Defence and certified by the Law Officer to be a person of legal knowledge and experience;

(b) The enquiry of such Military Courts or Committees into the cases of persons charged with any of the offences following, that is to say:

(I.) Taking part in or aiding and abetting any attack upon or using force against the National Forces;

(II.) Looting, arson, destruction, seizure, unlawful possession, or removal of or damage to any public or private property;

(III.) Having possession without proper authority of any bomb or article in the nature of a bomb, or any dynamite, gelignite, or other explosive substance, or any revolver, rifle, gun, or other firearm or lethal weapon, or any ammunition for any such firearm;

(IV.) The breach of any general order or regulation made by the Army authorities;

and the infliction by such Military Courts or Committees of the punishment of death, or of imprisonment for any period, or of a fine of any amount either with or without imprisonment, on any person found guilty by any such Court or Committee of any of the offences aforesaid;

(c) The removal by Army authorities of all or any person taken prisoner, arrested, or detained by the National forces to any place or places, whether within or without the area of jurisdiction of the Government, and the detention or imprisonment of any such persons in any place or places within or without the area aforesaid;

(d) The regulation and control of the sale, possession, transfer of, and dealing in revolvers, rifles, guns, and other firearms:

Now, this Dáil, being of opinion that the doing by the Army authorities of the several matters aforesaid is a matter of military necessity, doth hereby ratify and approve of the sanction given by the Government, and of the doing by the Army authorities of all or any of the acts and matters aforesaid.

Motion: 'That the Dáil do now adjourn', put and agreed to.

Source: http://oireachtasdebates.oireachtas.ie/debates authoring/debatesweb pack.nsf/takes/dail1922092600027?opendocument

APPENDIX 8

IN MEMORY OF SEÁN HALES

As the fall of an oak [in] the forest,
That had weathered the tempest for years,
As new pangs when the bosom is sorest
And the eyelids inflamed with their tears.
Such the void which our vision tomorrow,
Shall mourn in life's sorrowful vales,
Such the grief that shall deluge with sorrow,
Our land for the patriot Hales.

Like the drop of the eyelids in slumbers,
When the weary day draws to a close,
Like the sleep of a babe whom the numbers
Of a mother's song full to repose.
So when his fights with the Saxon were ended,
Their record shall history guard;
Our citizen soldier ascended
From earth to his Master's reward.

Round the hills where proud England's banner
Was oft brought to dust and the mire,
When the boys from Macroom and Liscannor

Scattered the Tans with their fire.
When our land was oppressed by the stranger,
And her glory enshrouded in night,
Seán was the foremost in danger,
He was always the van of the fight.

In the Dáil where our statesmen assemble,
With the calmness of wisdom his voice,
Never schooled in the art to dissemble,
Ever prompt with the right to rejoice,
Has been heard, and the eloquent stories
That he told of his country we have,
Though the voice that depicted her glories
Is silent and mute in the grave.

Struck down in the noonday of life,
In the city that cradled Sinn Féin;
To succour the cause of dissension and strife
They pierced the brave heart of Shane.
He who over the mountain and valley
Harassed our foes by night and by day.
While his clarion voice would rally
His column again to the fray.

Let him sleep where Southern grass tosses,
Its green foliage over his grave,

Though Cork and the nation lament their losses;
All the world mourns the death of the brave.
Let him sleep in the breast of his dear land,
Wrapped in the sward from his own native dales,
For the fame of his valour shall garland
With glory the tomb of Seán Hales.

Words by David Ryan, Caherconlish.
Courtesy of Anne Hales

ENDNOTES

1 EARLY YEARS

1   The Irish Republican Brotherhood (IRB) was established on St Patrick's Day, 17 March 1858, in Dublin by James Stephens. Stephens had been a member of the Young Ireland movement, which in 1848 had asserted Ireland's right to independence by force of arms in Ballingarry, County Tipperary. The rebellion failed, but Stephens was determined to strike another blow and set up the Brotherhood. It was a secret organisation, the only aim of which was to win full independence by any means necessary. A Military Council within the IRB planned the Easter Rising, and its members were executed in the aftermath of the Rising in Kilmainham Gaol in May 1916.

2   William O'Brien (1852–1928) was born in Mallow, County Cork. He was a journalist and was greatly influenced by both the Fenian movement (IRB) and the plight of tenant farmers. He was a member of the IRB but resigned as he believed that the same objectives could be achieved through political means. He was a supporter of Charles Stewart Parnell, who was so impressed by O'Brien's ideas that he appointed him editor of *The United Irishman*, the journal of the Land League. He was imprisoned during the Land War and while incarcerated wrote the 'No Rent Manifesto', which encouraged tenant farmers to not pay their rent in order to highlight their conditions. He was elected to the House of Commons as an MP. In 1898 he co-founded the United Irish League (UIL), its aim being political and social reform, rights for tenant farmers and self-government.

It was a popular organisation but due to differences with some members he then formed the All for Ireland League. Always a believer in the rights of tenant farmers to own their land, he believed that through financial support from the government it would be possible for the farmers to achieve this.

3   *The Cork Examiner,* 23 August 1902; 20 June 1907.

4   Tom Hales, Military Archives, Bureau of Military History (BMH) Witness Statement (WS) 20, p. 1.

5   *The Cork Examiner,* 22 May 1907.

6   *Ibid.*

7   The ICA was established on 23 November 1913 during the Dublin Lockout, in response to the terrible treatment that the workers who were out on strike were enduring at the hands of the police. Founded by Jack White, Jim Larkin and James Connolly, it was a small body of men, and later women, who not only wished to protect the workers but also wanted to gain decent living conditions for the working class and, under Connolly's leadership, hoped to establish a Workers' Republic. In response to the formation of the Ulster Volunteer Force (UVF) in 1913 to resist the introduction of Home Rule, the Irish Volunteers were founded in Dublin on 25 November 1913 to ensure its introduction. Cumann na mBan (The Irishwomen's Council) was founded in Wynn's Hotel, Dublin in April 1914. Before the formation of Cumann na mBan, a women's organisation had existed since 1900: Inghinidhe na hÉireann (Daughters of Ireland). Founded by Maud Gonne, Inghinidhe was a revolutionary women's organisation promoting Irish independence, the production of Irish goods and the education of the poorer classes. Inghinidhe was based solely in Dublin and with the advent of a national organisation such as the Irish Volunteers, it was decided that a new, much larger organisation

for women should be formed to work with these nationalist bodies. Inghinidhe was amalgamated into Cumann na mBan and became a branch of the organisation based on the south side of Dublin city and attached to the Third and Fourth Battalions of the Dublin Brigade, Irish Volunteers.

8   McDonnell was a local Bandon businessman. For a more detailed account of William Keyes McDonnell's role in the movement, see Kathleen Keyes McDonnell, *There is a Bridge at Bandon* (Cork 1972).

9   Interview with Seán Hales, author's collection.

10   Their three other sisters, Annie, Bessie and Hannah, were not involved. Annie died in 1911, Hannah died in 1923 and Bessie suffered with ill health for most of her life.

11   The Irish Volunteers were set up along the same lines as the British Army. There was an Executive which oversaw the whole organisation, with individual brigades for different counties (for example, the Dublin Brigade and Cork Brigade), with a commandant in overall charge of each. Prior to the Easter Rising the brigades were made up of battalions. Each battalion was made up of a number of companies, and a company was made up of sections, usually based on a particular locality. With the reorganisation after the Rising, and the increase in membership, this was no longer feasible and in some cases a brigade was divided. For example, Cork was divided into three brigades, although each commandant would have to report to their superior officer, who in this case would have been Tomás MacCurtain and later Terence MacSwiney.

12   McDonnell, *There is a Bridge at Bandon*, p. 35.

13   'The History of the Sinn Féin Movement in West Cork 1915–1918', Dorothy Price Papers, MS 15,344, National Library of Ireland.

14   Tom Hales, BMH WS 20, p. 2.

15   Jeremiah O'Donovan Rossa was from Rosscarbery and a veteran Fenian. After his imprisonment in the 1860s he was exiled to America, where he played a prominent role in Clan na Gael, the American wing of the IRB. His death in July 1915 was seen by many in the IRB, especially Tom Clarke, as an opportunity to raise the profile of the Volunteer movement. A committee was established to organise the repatriation of O'Donovan Rossa's body back to Ireland. Thousands queued to pay their respects as he lay in state in Dublin's City Hall. Crowds of people lined the streets to witness the funeral procession as it made its way to Glasnevin Cemetery where Patrick Pearse gave his famous oration at the graveside. O'Donovan Rossa's funeral was a huge publicity coup for the IRB leadership. Many in the Volunteers and Cumann na mBan credit that event for making them decide to join the Republican movement.

16   *The Southern Star,* 12 April 1952.

17   The companies were Ballinadee, Kilpatrick, Clogagh, Lyre, Bandon, Ballinhassig and Aiohill, in total approximately 400 men.

2 EASTER RISING

1   Tom Hales, BMH WS 20, p. 3.

2   William Hales, 'Easter Week, 1916 and the Ballinadee Battalion, Irish Volunteers', *Bandon Historical Journal,* No. 17 (2001), p. 28.

3   Due to the failure to land German arms in Kerry, the arrest of Roger Casement and the secrecy involved in the planning of the Rising, Eoin MacNeill issued a countermanding order that no manoeuvres would take place on Easter Sunday.

4   Tom Hales, BMH WS 20, p. 4.

5   William Hales, 'Easter Week, 1916 and the Ballinadee Battalion, Irish Volunteers', *Bandon Historical Journal*, No. 17 (2001), p. 49.

6   *Ibid.*, p. 50.

7   *Ibid.*

8   *Ibid.*

9   Tom Hales, BMH WS 20, p. 4.

10 The agreement to surrender arms had been reached between the Brigade HQ and the authorities. An amnesty was to be granted to those Volunteers who handed over their weapons. The reprieve was not honoured and a number of men were arrested soon after as a result.

11 'The History of the Sinn Féin Movement in West Cork 1915–1918', Dorothy Price Papers; John Corkery, BMH WS 41, p. 1.

12 *The Southern Star*, 24 May 1952.

13 Tom Hales, BMH WS 20, p. 4.

14 *Ibid.*, p. 5. Two other men, Paddy Hyde and John Roche, were also captured at Knocknacurra.

15 Daniel Hegarty, BMH WS 33, pp. 3–4.

16 *Irish Times 1916 Rebellion Handbook* (Belfast 1998), p. 82.

17 *Ibid.*, p. 89.

18 This refers to the title of Sean O'Mahony's book, *Frongoch: University of Revolution* (Dublin 1995). Over 1,800 men were interned in the camp in the aftermath of the Rising and while interned they were determined to use their imprisonment to their advantage. They reorganised themselves on a military footing, with a camp commandant and a full military staff

which organised their daily routine, including lectures in Irish history, the Irish language and military drill. Commandant W. J. Brennan-Whitmore, who had fought in North Earl Street during the Rising and was the camp adjutant, referred to the camp as a military academy in his book *With the Irish in Frongoch* (Dublin 1917 [reprinted 2013]). And in July 1916 Sidney Gifford-Czira referred to the internees who had been released at that time as 'graduates', and those still in custody as taking a 'post-graduate course'.

19   In his last message to the Irish people, given to his wife, Kathleen, on the eve of his execution in Kilmainham Gaol, Tom Clarke stated that although the Rising had failed, it was the first successful blow against the British that would eventually lead to full freedom. For the complete speech, see Kathleen Clarke, *Revolutionary Woman* (Dublin 2008), p. 139.

20   O'Mahony, *Frongoch: University of Revolution*, p. 61.

21   Frank Hardiman, BMH WS 406, p. 22.

22   With the executions of the leaders of the Easter Rising, it was imperative that the IRB reorganise if it was to further its objectives. Tom Clarke had given his wife, Kathleen, the names of men she was to contact to begin this work, which she succeeded in doing.

23   O'Mahony, *Frongoch: University of Revolution*, pp. 66–7.

24   KMGLM 2012.0015, Kilmainham Gaol Archives.

25   Letter from Seán Hales to William McDonnell, Bandon, 30 August 1916, courtesy of Éamon de Burca.

26   *Ibid.*

27   For a more detailed account of the role Frongoch played in the national movement, see Brennan-Whitmore, *With the Irish in*

Frongoch; Lyn Ebenezer, *Frongoch and the Birth of the IRA* (Wales 2006); O'Mahony, *Frongoch: University of Revolution.*

3   HOMECOMING AND REORGANISATION

1   *The Southern Star,* 23 August 1952.

2   *Ibid.*

3   Tom Hales, BMH WS 20, p. 5.

4   'The History of the Sinn Féin Movement in West Cork 1915–1918', Dorothy Price Papers.

5   Letter from Robert Hales to Count Plunkett, 4 May 1917. Count Plunkett Collection, MS 11,383(6), National Library of Ireland.

6   Letter from Seán Hales to Count Plunkett, 9 May 1917. Count Plunkett Collection, MS 11,383(6), National Library of Ireland.

7   The companies that made up the Bandon Battalion were Ballinadee, Bandon, Kilbrittain, Innishannon, Clogagh, Crosspound, Farnivane and Newcestown.

8   For full details of these activities, see 'The History of the Sinn Féin Movement in West Cork 1915–1918', Dorothy Price Papers; Liam Deasy, *Towards Ireland Free* (Cork 1973), pp. 18–25.

9   On 12 April 1918 Joseph Dowling, a member of Roger Casement's Irish Brigade, was arrested off the coast of Galway. He had been sent by the German government to make contact with Sinn Féin, but few people knew of this. The authorities saw it as their chance to wipe out the Sinn Féin leadership and with little, if any, evidence they carried out their arrests.

10   'The History of the Sinn Féin Movement in West Cork 1915–1918', Dorothy Price Papers.

11   *Ibid.*

12   William Hales, BMH WS 666, pp. 4–6.

13   For further details of the escape, see 'The History of the Sinn Féin Movement in West Cork 1915–1918', Dorothy Price Papers; Deasy, *Towards Ireland Free*, pp. 21–2.

14   'The History of the Sinn Féin Movement in West Cork 1915–1918', Dorothy Price Papers.

15   The companies were Timoleague, Ballinadee, Bandon, Newcestown, Crosspound, Kilbrittain, Ballinspittle, Barryroe, Quarry Cross, Mount Pleasant, Clogagh, Innishannon and Kilpatrick.

16   It was also known as Cork No. 3 Brigade. Cork No. 1 Brigade was under the command of Tomás MacCurtain, and later Seán O'Hegarty, and Liam Lynch was in command of Cork No. 2 Brigade. The battalions were Bandon (1st), Clonakilty (2nd), Dunmanway (3rd), Skibbereen (4th), Bantry (5th) and Castletownbere (6th).

17   See Appendix 2.

4   1919–1920: FIGHTING FOR INDEPENDENCE

1   For full details, see Cornelius Flynn, 'My Part in Irish Independence', *Bandon Historical Journal*, No. 4 (1988), pp. 60–1; Daniel Donovan, BMH WS 1608, pp. 3–4.

2   Seán Crowley, *From Newce to Truce* (Cork, no date), pp. 299–300.

3   *Ibid.*, pp. 233, 393–4.

4   McDonnell, *There is a Bridge at Bandon*, p. 150.

5   Daniel Donovan, BMH WS 1608, pp. 5–6.

6   Statement by Tom Hales regarding his torture by the Essex Regiment, Donal Hales Papers, U53, Cork Archives Institute; see Appendix 3.

7   *Ibid.*

8   *Ibid.*

9   *Ibid.*

10   *Ibid.*

11   *Ibid.* The American Commission on Conditions in Ireland was established to find out the truth about what was happening in Ireland.

12   National Archives, Dáil Éireann Local Government Records, DELG 2/453.

13   *Ibid.*

14   *Ibid.*

15   For details of the ambush, see Crowley, *From Newce to Truce*, pp. 225, 261; Deasy, *Towards Ireland Free*, pp. 135–6; McDonnell, *There is a Bridge at Bandon*, pp. 171–2.

16   John Lordan was captain of the Newcestown Company and was later a member of the brigade flying column.

17   For details of the Newcestown ambush, see Crowley, *From Newce to Truce*, pp. 307–14, 368–70, 400; Deasy, *Towards Ireland Free*, pp. 144–6; McDonnell, *There is a Bridge at Bandon*, pp. 178–9; Daniel Donovan, BMH WS 1608, pp. 7–8.

18   For details of the Toureen ambush, see Tom Barry, *Guerilla Days in Ireland* (Dublin 1997), pp. 28–31; Deasy, *Towards Ireland Free*, pp. 154–6; Crowley, *From Newce to Truce*, pp. 287–8.

19   Deasy, *Towards Ireland Free*, pp. 163–5.

20   Daniel Donovan, BMH WS 1608, p. 8.

21   Meda Ryan, *Michael Collins and the Women in His Life* (Cork 1996), p. 77.

22   Donal Hales, BMH WS 292, p. 1.

23 *Ibid.*, p. 2.

24 Seán Ó Séaghdha, BMH WS 760, pp. 2–3.

25 Donal Hales, BMH WS 292, pp. 7–8.

5 JANUARY–JULY 1921

1 For details, see Daniel Donovan, BMH WS 1608, p. 9; Barry, *Guerilla Days in Ireland*, p. 65.

2 Deasy, *Towards Ireland Free*, p. 196.

3 *Ibid.*, pp. 201–2; Barry, *Guerilla Days in Ireland*, pp. 68–73; Cornelius Flynn, 'My Part in Irish Independence', *Bandon Historical Journal*, No. 4 (1988), pp. 55–70.

4 Daniel Donovan, BMH WS 1608, p. 12. Each section actually contained fourteen men.

5 Barry, *Guerilla Days in Ireland*, p. 128.

6 Deasy, *Towards Ireland Free*, p. 239.

7 Those killed were Volunteers Peter Monaghan, Jeremiah O'Leary and Con Daly. Volunteers Dan Corcoran and Jim Crowley were wounded.

8 Diarmuid Begley, *The Road to Crossbarry* (Cork 2002), p. 96. Understandably the numbers of those killed and wounded during the ambush varied considerably according to both the British and Republican accounts of the ambush. The figure quoted is from the Republican side, but British reports at the time quoted ten men killed, three wounded and six IRA killed. According to newspaper reports at the time, the actual casualties of the British forces were nine dead and seven wounded. The dead soldiers were Driver Baker, Private Cawley, Private Crofer, Driver Gray, Constable Kenward, Driver Martin, Private Steward, Sergeant Watts and Private Wilkins. Wounded:

Sergeant Loftus, Lieutenant Hotblack, Lance Corporal Orpin, Constable Rennie, Private Sayer, Lieutenant Towers and Lance Corporal White.

9   For full details of the Crossbarry ambush, see Barry, *Guerilla Days in Ireland*, pp. 122–31; Deasy, *Towards Ireland Free*, pp. 231–54; Begley, *The Road to Crossbarry*, pp. 74–97; Daniel Donovan, BMH WS 1608, pp. 11–14; Denis Lordan, BMH WS 470, pp. 20–4.

10 Barry, *Guerilla Days in Ireland*, p. 153.

11 For full details of the attack on Rosscarbery Barracks, see Uinseann MacEoin, *Survivors* (Dublin 1980), interview with Tom Kelleher, pp. 227–9; Barry, *Guerilla Days in Ireland*, pp. 142–53; Denis Lordan, BMH WS 470, pp. 25–6.

12 Daniel Donovan, BMH WS 1608, p. 15.

13 Martial law was introduced during the Easter Rising, which meant that the military took control of what would usually be the work of the civilian administration of the British government. It was again introduced to many parts of Ireland in early 1918 in order to quell the rise of Sinn Féin and the Republican movement. Sinn Féin and all nationalist and Republican bodies were proclaimed illegal organisations, it was illegal to carry a hurley, which could be seen as a weapon, and meetings and assemblies were also declared illegal, with anyone participating in these activities liable to be arrested. As the War of Independence escalated, the military were granted more powers, including the power to try and execute those whom they considered to be suspect individuals.

14 Cornelius Flynn, 'My Part in Irish Independence', *Bandon Historical Journal*, No. 4 (1988), p. 69. Bill Hales is William Hales.

15 Deasy, *Towards Ireland Free*, pp. 283–8.

16 *Ibid.*, pp. 292–3.

17 Conor J. Morrissey, 'The Earl of Bandon and the Burning of Castle Bernard, June 1921', *Bandon Historical Journal*, No. 27 (2011), p. 34.

18 Denis Lordan, BMH WS 470, p. 30.

19 *Ibid.*

20 Conor J. Morrissey, 'The Earl of Bandon and the Burning of Castle Bernard, June 1921', *Bandon Historical Journal*, No. 27 (2011), p. 39.

21 *Ibid.*, p. 40.

22 Donal Hales, BMH WS 292, p. 8.

6 **TRUCE AND TREATY**

1 Kenneth Griffith and Timothy E. O'Grady, *Curious Journey: An Oral History of Ireland's Unfinished Revolution* (London 1982), p. 234.

2 *Ibid.*, p. 247.

3 *The Southern Star*, 30 August 1952.

4 *Irish Independent*, 24 December 1921.

5 Letter from Seán Hales to Donal Hales, 2 October 1921, Donal Hales Papers, U53, Cork Archives Institute.

6 The British delegation included Prime Minister David Lloyd George, Lord Birkenhead, Winston Churchill, Austin Chamberlain, L. Worthington Evans, Hamar Greenwood and Gordon Hewart.

7 Ryan, *Michael Collins and the Women in His Life*, pp. 119–20.

8 *Irish Independent*, 24 December 1921.

9   Parliamentary Debates Official Report, Private Session, Dáil Éireann, Vol. T, No. 5, 17 December 1921.

10   Parliamentary Debates Official Report, Public Session, Dáil Éireann, Vol. T, No. 15, 7 January 1922.

11   Liam Deasy, *Brother Against Brother* (Cork 1998), p. 32.

7 DIVISION

1   Maryann Valiulis, *Portrait of a Revolutionary: General Richard Mulcahy and the Founding of the Irish Free State* (Dublin 1992), p. 122.

2   The IRA had come under the authority of the Dáil in 1919 as the legitimate army of the Republic. As such, every member of the IRA had to swear an oath of allegiance to the Dáil recognising it as the legitimate government of the Irish Republic.

3   Deasy, *Brother Against Brother,* pp. 35–6.

4   For more details on the Limerick crisis, see Pádraig Óg Ó Ruairc, *The Battle for Limerick City* (Cork 2010).

5   Valiulis, *Portrait of a Revolutionary,* pp. 138–9.

6   The other fourteen members were Liam Lynch, Liam Mellows, Joseph McKelvey, Rory O'Connor, Florrie O'Donoghue, Ernie O'Malley, Seán Moylan, Frank Barrett, Michael Kilroy, Peadar O'Donnell, Joseph O'Connor, Séamus Robinson, Seán O'Hegarty and P. J. Ruttledge.

7   *The Southern Star,* 18 March 1922.

8   *Ibid.,* 8 April 1922.

9   J. J. Bradley, BMH WS 190. p. 16.

10   Liz Gillis, *The Fall of Dublin* (Cork 2011), p. 26.

11   As part of the Treaty agreement, a general election had to be

called in which the Irish people had the opportunity to vote on the issue of the Treaty. The date set for the election was 16 June 1922.

12 Letter from Seán O'Hegarty to Liam Mellows, 11 April 1922, Florence O'Donoghue Papers, MS 31,186, National Library of Ireland.

13 For more details supporting that argument, see Peter Hart, *The I.R.A. and Its Enemies: Violence and Community in Cork 1916–1923* (Oxford 1999); also, Gerard Murphy, *The Year of Disappearances: Political Killings in Cork 1921–1922* (Dublin 2010).

14 For more on the counter-argument, see Barry Keane, *Massacre in West Cork: The Dunmanway and Ballygroman Killings* (Cork 2014).

15 Meda Ryan, *Tom Barry: IRA Freedom Fighter* (Cork 2003), p. 161.

16 *The Irish Press*, 30 June 1936.

8   ATTEMPTS AT UNITY

1 For more details, see Gillis, *The Fall of Dublin*, pp. 28–31.

2 *Irish Independent*, 15 April 1922.

3 Eoin Neeson, *The Civil War in Ireland 1921–23* (Dublin 1995), pp. 227–8.

4 Gillis, *The Fall of Dublin*, p. 142.

5 *Ibid.*

6 *Ibid.*, p. 37.

7 After the takeover of the Four Courts, the anti-Treaty IRA also took over Kilmainham Gaol, Dublin Port and Docks Offices, the Kildare Street Club and Messrs Lever Bros. The Freemason's Hall in Molesworth Street was used to house the Belfast

refugees. Since 1920 there had been a huge increase in attacks on nationalists, most notably in Belfast and Lisburn, by members of the unionist community with the backing of the authorities. The violence escalated to such an extent that numerous houses were burned down in these communities. Fearing for their safety, many thousands came to Dublin to seek refuge.

8   Gillis, *The Fall of Dublin*, p. 39.

9   THIRD ARMY CONVENTION AND CIVIL WAR

1   For more details on the convention, see Florence O'Donoghue, *No Other Law* (Dublin 1986), pp. 245–6; Neeson, *The Civil War in Ireland 1921–1923*, p. 65.

2   The Executive forces had nothing to do with the shooting of Wilson. It has been suggested that it was a previous order from Michael Collins during the War of Independence, as Wilson was one of the main protagonists in the pogroms against the nationalists in the Six Counties at the time. The order it seems was never rescinded. Despite many strenuous efforts made by Collins to save Dunne and O'Sullivan, both men were hanged on 10 August 1922 in Wandsworth Prison for the assassination.

3   For more details, see Deasy, *Brother Against Brother*, pp. 48–9; O'Donoghue, *No Other Law*, pp. 259–60.

4   Deasy, *Brother Against Brother*, p. 52.

10   BROTHERS AT WAR

1   Coppeen Papers, A/0991/2, Lot 3, 7 August 1922, Military Archives.

2   Griffith and O'Grady, *Curious Journey*, pp. 288–9.

3   *Ibid.*

4   *Ibid.*, p. 290.

5   Deasy, *Brother Against Brother*, pp. 72–3.

6   Griffith and O'Grady, *Curious Journey*, p. 290.

7   Coppeen Papers, A/0991/5, Lot 3, 6 July 1922, Military Archives.

8   *Ibid.*, A/0991/4, Lot 3, 13 July 1922.

9   *Ibid.*, 19 July 1922.

10   Griffith and O'Grady, *Curious Journey*, pp. 290–1.

11   Coppeen Papers, A/0991/3, Lot 3, 6 September 22, Military Archives.

12   Michael Hopkinson, *Green Against Green: The Irish Civil War* (Dublin 1988), pp. 164–5.

11   THE DEATH OF COLLINS

1   Arthur Griffith died of a cerebral haemorrhage. He was fifty-one years old.

2   Hopkinson, *Green Against Green*, pp. 176–7.

3   Tomás Ó Maoileóin, alias Seán Forde, was a member of the Irish Volunteers from their inception in 1913. He fought in the Easter Rising and during the War of Independence in Limerick. He was arrested in 1920 and taken to Spike Island. He successfully escaped in 1921. He refused to accept the Treaty. For more details on Ó Maoileóin, see MacEoin, *Survivors*, pp. 75–104.

4   *Ibid.*, p. 99.

5   O'Donoghue was a prominent member of Cork No. 1 Brigade during the War of Independence. He, together with Seán O'Hegarty, O/C Cork No. 1 Brigade during that time, was neutral. The two later set up the Neutral IRA Association to try to end the Civil War.

6   John M. Feehan, *The Shooting of Michael Collins: Murder or Accident?* (Cork 1991), p. 52.

7   Deasy, *Brother Against Brother*, p. 77.

8   Meda Ryan, *The Day Michael Collins Was Shot* (Dublin 1998), p. 74.

9   For more details on the events of the day, see Ryan, *The Day Michael Collins Was Shot*, pp. 79–89.

10 *Ibid.*, p. 90.

11 For more details, see Feehan, *The Shooting of Michael Collins*, p. 56.

12 Ryan, *The Day Michael Collins Was Shot*, p. 91.

13 *Ibid.*, p. 74.

14 Deasy, *Brother Against Brother*, p. 78.

15 *Ibid.*, pp. 78–9.

16 Ryan, *The Day Michael Collins Was Shot*, p. 95.

17 *Ibid.*, p. 97.

18 *Ibid.*, p. 105.

19 *Ibid.*, p. 109.

20 For a more detailed account of Collins' death, see Deasy, *Brother Against Brother*; Feehan, *The Shooting of Michael Collins*; Hopkinson, *Green Against Green*; Ryan, *The Day Michael Collins Was Shot*; Rex Taylor, *Michael Collins: The Big Fellow* (London 1958).

21 Ryan, *The Day Michael Collins Was Shot*, p. 127.

22 For a full list of those present, see Deasy, *Brother Against Brother*, pp. 79–80.

23 *Ibid.*

12   SUSPICION, ARREST AND ASSASSINATION

1   Griffith and O'Grady, *Curious Journey*, p. 297.

2   Ryan, *The Day Michael Collins Was Shot*, p. 92.

3   *Ibid.*, pp. 31–2.

4   *The Freeman's Journal*, 25 August 1922.

5   *Ibid.*

6   Ryan, *The Day Michael Collins Was Shot*, pp. 198–9.

7   *Ibid.*, p. 144.

8   *Ibid.*, pp. 142–5.

9   Feehan, *The Shooting of Michael Collins*, p. 111.

10   *The Southern Star*, 23 September 1922.

11   See Appendix 7.

12   Civil War Internment Database, Military Archives.

13   I am indebted to Brendan Kelly for giving me access to his unpublished manuscript relating to his father Paddy's experiences as a member of the pro-Treaty forces in the Civil War.

14   *Irish Independent*, 24 November 1922.

15   Civil War Internment Database, Military Archives.

16   Feehan, *The Shooting of Michael Collins*, p. 111.

17   Vincent MacDowell, *Michael Collins and the Brotherhood* (Dublin 1997), p. 149.

18   Feehan, *The Shooting of Michael Collins*, p. 111.

19   Mícheal Ó Cuinneagáin, *On the Arm of Time* (Ireland 1992), pp. 116–22.

20   MacDowell, *Michael Collins and the Brotherhood*, p. 149.

21   Inquest on Seán Hales' death. Florence O'Donoghue Papers, MS 13,661, National Library of Ireland.

22   *The Southern Star,* 16 December 1922.

13   AFTERMATH

1   Donal Hales Papers, U53, Cork Archives Institute.

2   *Irish Independent,* 22 December 1922.

3   *The Cork Examiner,* 8 December 1922.

4   *Irish Independent,* 9 December 1922.

5   For Mulcahy's full response, see *Irish Independent,* 9 December 1922. This statement by Mulcahy is quite unusual when one considers that during the War of Independence Tomás MacCurtain, lord mayor of Cork, and Michael O'Callaghan, lord mayor of Limerick, were both shot and killed in their homes by crown forces in 1920 and 1921 respectively.

6   *The Southern Star,* 16 December 1922.

7   *The Cork Examiner,* 16 December 1922.

8   *Ibid.,* 11 December 1922.

9   *Irish Independent,* 22 December 1922.

10   Deasy, *Brother Against Brother,* pp. 93–4.

11   *An t-Óglach,* Vol. IV, No. 27, 16 December 1922.

12   For more details on the reprisal killings and executions, see Martin O'Dwyer, *Seventy-Seven of Mine Said Ireland* (Cashel 2006); Martin O'Dwyer, *Death before Dishonour* (Cashel 2010); Dorothy Macardle, *Tragedies of Kerry* (Dublin 1924); James Durney, *The Civil War in Kildare* (Cork 2011).

13   James Durney, 'The Curragh Internees, 1921–21: From Defiance to Defeat', *Journal of the County Kildare Archaeological Society and Surrounding District,* Vol. XX, Pt 2 (2010–11), p. 14.

14   *Daily Sheet,* No. 4, 29 October 1923, Fintan Murphy Collection, CD 227/34/B3, Military Archives.

15   Seán Hales Personal File, A Series Papers, A/7749, Military Archives.

14   CONCLUSION

1   *The Irish Times*, 8 December 1922.

2   Florence O'Donoghue Papers, 27 January 1923, MS 31,242, National Library of Ireland.

3   *Sunday Independent*, 17 February 2002.

4   Letter from Madge Hales to Donal Hales, 9 June 1923, Donal Hales Papers, U53, Cork Archives Institute.

5   Letter to *The Cork Examiner*, 11 December 1922, Donal Hales Papers, U53, Cork Archives Institute.

6   Letter from Madge Hales to Donal Hales, 1 December 1925, Donal Hales Papers, U53, Cork Archives Institute.

7   *Ibid.*, 9 June 1923.

8   *The Southern Star*, 16 December 1922.

APPENDIX 3

1   This is an American report and American spellings have been left unamended.

APPENDIX 5

1   *Franc-tireur* is a French term for a guerrilla or irregular soldier.

2   The *Irish Bulletin* was the weekly Republican newspaper produced by the Department of Publicity, under the control of Desmond FitzGerald and later Erskine Childers. Reports of engagements with the crown forces and reprisals by the British military were collected and compiled into weekly editions, which were

printed in Dublin. These were then distributed not just in Ireland but throughout Europe through the many Republican Envoys located there, including Donal Hales in Italy. The purpose of such a publication was to report what was happening from the Irish point of view, which could not be done in the mainstream newspapers due to restrictions from the authorities.

3   Third and 3rd are used inconsistently in the original text and these have been left to reflect the original source.

BIBLIOGRAPHY

MANUSCRIPTS
Dublin
Military Archives
A Series Papers
Bureau of Military History Witness Statements (BMH WS)
Military Service Pension Files
Civil War Internment Database
Contemporary Documents
Coppeen Papers
Fintan Murphy Collection

National Library
Florence O'Donoghue Papers
Count Plunkett Papers
Dorothy Price Papers

National Archives
Dáil Éireann Local Government Records (DELG)
Census Returns 1901 and 1911
Colonial Office (CO) Files

Kilmainham Gaol
Autograph Books

Cork
Cork Archives Institute
Donal Hales Papers

GOVERNMENT PUBLICATIONS
Official Report: Debate on the Treaty Between Great Britain and Ireland
(Talbot Press, Dublin)

JOURNALS
Bandon Historical Journal
Journal of the County Kildare Archaeological Society and Surrounding District

INTERVIEWS
Seán Hales, Bandon, recorded September 2004

NEWSPAPERS
An t-Óglach
Cork Examiner, The
Freeman's Journal, The
Irish Bulletin
Irish Independent
Irish Press, The
Irish Times, The
Southern Star, The
Sunday Independent

PUBLISHED WORKS
Ballineen and Enniskeane Heritage Group, *Dick Barrett (1889–1922): His Life and Death* (Cork 1997)
Barrett, J. J., *In the Name of the Game* (The Dub Press, Wicklow 1997)
Barry, Tom, *Guerilla Days in Ireland* (Anvil Books, Dublin 1997)
Begley, Diarmuid, *The Road to Crossbarry* (2nd edn, Deso Publications, Cork 2002)

Blake, Francis M., *The Irish Civil War and What it Still Means for the Irish People* (Information on Ireland, London 1986)

Brady, Conor, *Guardians of the Peace* (Prendeville Publishing Ltd, London 2000)

Brennan-Whitmore, W. J., *With the Irish in Frongoch* (Talbot Press, Dublin 1917)

Clarke, Kathleen, *Revolutionary Woman* (O'Brien Press, Dublin 2008)

Coogan, Tim Pat, *Michael Collins: A Biography* (Hutchinson, London 1990)

Crowley, Seán, *From Newce to Truce* (Cork, no date)

Deasy, Liam, *Towards Ireland Free* (Royal Carbery Books, Cork 1973)

— *Brother Against Brother* (Mercier Press, Cork 1998)

Dolan, Anne, *Commemorating the Irish Civil War: History & Memory, 1923–2000* (Cambridge University Press, Cambridge 2006)

Durney, James, *The Civil War in Kildare* (Mercier Press, Cork 2011)

Ebenezer, Lyn, *Frongoch and the Birth of the IRA* (1st edn, Gwasg Carreg Gwalch, Wales 2006)

Feehan, John M., *The Shooting of Michael Collins: Murder or Accident* (Royal Carbery Books, Cork 1991)

Gillis, Liz, *The Fall of Dublin* (Mercier Press, Cork 2011)

Griffith, Kenneth and O'Grady, Timothy E., *Curious Journey: An Oral History of Ireland's Unfinished Revolution* (Hutchinson, London 1982)

Hart, Peter, *The I.R.A. and Its Enemies: Violence and Community in Cork 1916–1923* (Oxford University Press, Oxford 1999)

Hopkinson, Michael, *Green Against Green: The Irish Civil War* (Gill & Macmillan, Dublin 1988)

— *The Irish War of Independence* (Gill & Macmillan, Dublin 2004)

Irish Times 1916 Rebellion Handbook (Mourne River Press, Belfast 1998)

Keane, Barry, *Massacre in West Cork: The Dunmanway and Ballygroman Killings* (Mercier Press, Cork 2014)

Kilmichael & Crossbarry Commemoration Committee, *The Wild Heather Glen: The Kilmichael Story of Grief and Glory* (Cork 2005)

Macardle, Dorothy, *Tragedies of Kerry* (Emton Press, Dublin 1924)

— *The Irish Republic* (Irish Press Ltd, Dublin 1951)

MacDowell, Vincent, *Michael Collins and the Brotherhood* (Ashfield Press, Dublin 1997)

MacEoin, Uinseann, *Survivors* (1st edn, Argenta Publications, Dublin 1980)

McDonnell, Kathleen Keyes, *There is a Bridge at Bandon* (Mercier Press, Cork 1972)

Mulcahy, Ristéard, *Richard Mulcahy (1886–1971): A Family Memoir* (Aurelian Press, Dublin 1999)

Murphy, Gerard, *The Year of Disappearances: Political Killings in Cork 1921–1922* (1st edn, Gill & Macmillan, Dublin 2010)

Neeson, Eoin, *The Civil War in Ireland 1921–1923* (Poolbeg Press, Dublin 1995)

Ó Cuinneagáin, Mícheal, *On the Arm of Time* (Ronan Press, Donegal 1992)

O'Donnell, Peadar, *The Gates Flew Open* (Mercier Press, Cork 1965)

O'Donoghue, Florence, *No Other Law* (Anvil Books, Dublin 1986)

O'Dwyer, Martin, *Seventy-Seven of Mine Said Ireland* (Deshaoirse, Cashel 2006)

— *Death Before Dishonour* (Cashel 2010)

O'Hegarty, P. S., *The Victory of Sinn Féin* (University College Dublin Press, Dublin 1998)

O'Mahony, Sean, *Frongoch: University of Revolution* (FDR Teoranta, Dublin 1995)

Ó Ruairc, Pádraig Óg, *The Battle for Limerick City* (Mercier Press, Cork 2010)

Ryan, Meda, *Michael Collins and the Women in His Life* (Mercier Press, Cork 1996)

— *The Day Michael Collins Was Shot* (Poolbeg Press, Dublin 1998)

— *Tom Barry: IRA Freedom Fighter* (Mercier Press, Cork 2003)

Taylor, Rex, *Michael Collins: The Big Fellow* (Hutchinson, London 1958)

Valiulis, Maryann, *Portrait of a Revolutionary: General Richard Mulcahy and the Founding of the Irish Free State* (Irish Academic Press, Dublin 1992)

Younger, Calton, *Ireland's Civil War* (Fontana Books, Britain 1968)

INDEX